THE ECONOMICS OF PUBLIC-PRIVATE PARTNERSHIPS

In the past 25 years, many developing and advanced economies have introduced public-private partnerships (PPPs), which bundle finance, construction, and operation into a long-term contract with a private firm. In this book, the authors provide a summary of what, they believe, are the main lessons learned from the interplay of experience and the academic literature on PPPs, addressing such key issues as when governments should choose a PPP instead of a conventional provision, how PPPs should be implemented, and the appropriate governance structures for PPPs. The authors argue that the fiscal impact of PPPs is similar to that of conventional provisions and that they do not liberate public funds. The case for PPPs rests on efficiency gains and service improvements, which often prove elusive. Indeed, pervasive renegotiations, faulty fiscal accounting, and poor governance threaten the PPP model.

Eduardo Engel is professor of economics at the University of Chile and visiting professor at Yale University. He is a Fellow of the Econometric Society and was awarded the society's Frisch Medal in 2002. He has published in leading academic journals, such as the *American Economic Review*, *Econometrica*, the *Journal of Political Economy*, and the *Quarterly Journal of Economics*. He holds a PhD in economics from Massachusetts Institute of Technology, a PhD in statistics from Stanford University, and an engineering degree from the University of Chile.

Ronald D. Fischer is professor of economics in the industrial engineering department of Universidad de Chile in Santiago. His research is on the economics of public-private partnerships; the link between financial market inefficiencies and economic performance; and the economics of regulated industries, especially seaports. He has published widely in leading academic journals, including the *Journal of Political Economy* and the *Quarterly Journal of Economics*. He holds a PhD in economics from the University of Pennsylvania.

Alexander Galetovic is professor of economics at Universidad de los Andes in Santiago, Chile. His research is on the economics of public-private partnerships, the determinants of equilibrium industry structure, and the economics of electricity. He has published in leading economics journals, including the *Journal of Political Economy*, the *Review of Economics and Statistics*, the *Journal of the European Economic Association*, and the *Harvard Business Review*. He holds a PhD in economics from Princeton University.

The Economics of
Public-Private Partnerships

A Basic Guide

EDUARDO ENGEL

University of Chile

RONALD D. FISCHER

University of Chile

ALEXANDER GALETOVIC

Universidad de los Andes, Santiago, Chile

CAMBRIDGE
UNIVERSITY PRESS

CAMBRIDGE
UNIVERSITY PRESS

32 Avenue of the Americas, New York NY 10013-2473, USA

Cambridge University Press is part of the University of Cambridge.

It furthers the University's mission by disseminating knowledge in the pursuit of
education, learning and research at the highest international levels of excellence.

www.cambridge.org
Information on this title: www.cambridge.org/9781107035911

© Eduardo Engel, Ronald D. Fischer, and Alexander Galetovic 2014

First published 2014

A catalogue record for this publication is available from the British Library

Library of Congress Cataloguing in Publication data
Engel, Eduardo.
The Economics of public-private partnerships : a basic guide / Eduardo Engel,
University of Chile, Ronald D. Fischer, University of Chile, Alexander Galetovic,
Universidad de Los Andes, Santiago, Chile.
pages cm
Includes bibliographical references and index.
ISBN 978-1-107-03591-1 (hardback) – ISBN 978-1-107-63278-3 (paperback)
1. Public-private sector cooperation. I. Fischer, Ronald D.
II. Galetovic, Alexander. III. Title.
HD3871.E54 2014
338.8'7–dc23 2014011189

ISBN 978-1-107-03591-1 Hardback
ISBN 978-1-107-63278-3 Paperback

Contents

Tables

Figures

Preface

An important organizational form for providing infrastructure services has emerged in recent decades. Known as public-private partnerships or PPPs, this approach is often described as lying somewhere between public provision and privatization. In this book we provide a summary of what, we believe, are the main lessons arising from the interplay between experience and the academic literature on PPPs. What do we know that we did not know 10 or 20 years ago? What are the answers that experience combined with economic analysis provide to the question of choosing between PPPs and public provision? What is the best approach to design a PPP contract?

Until recently, infrastructure facilities such as highways, bridges, airports, schools, and jails were considered public goods. As such, they were built by governments, financed with taxes, and managed by public agencies. In the late 1980s, several countries began using PPPs. A PPP bundles finance, construction, and operation into a single long-term contract between the procurement authority and a private firm. During the life of the contract, the firm receives a stream of revenues as compensation for the initial investment, the operational costs, and the maintenance expenses. Depending on the contract, the stream of revenues may consist of user fees, payments from the procuring authority, or a combination of both. At the end of the contract, the assets revert to the government.

The importance of PPPs will likely continue to grow, albeit sometimes for the wrong reasons. Governments view PPPs as a costless means of releasing resources from infrastructure investment, which can then be redeployed to other programs. The deficiencies of fiscal accounting provide additional incentives to choose PPPs because they typically neither affect the budget deficit nor count as public debt. In addition, public provision of infrastructure is often deficient in quality and expensive, so PPPs promise the efficiency of private firms. The flaws of public provision – white elephants, pork-barrel projects, lack of transparency in public work contracts, and substandard maintenance and service quality – also give governments more reason to hope that PPPs will provide better performance and service quality.

A notorious aspect of the experience with PPP contracts is that they are routinely renegotiated. Some renegotiations are to be expected because these are long-term contracts and circumstances change over the life of a concession. However, there is extensive evidence showing that renegotiations often take place shortly after the awarding of the contract, under terms that favor the concessionaire. Renegotiations cast doubt on the alleged benefits of PPPs. They lead to adverse selection problems because they attract firms with a comparative advantage in lobbying but relatively less skill in building and operating facilities. Furthermore, they weaken the incentives for governments to design and select projects with care and reduce firms' incentives to contain costs, the moral hazard problem. Finally, they provide political incumbents with yet another means of anticipating spending.

In this book we show that it is possible to be more precise about the extent to which PPPs are akin to public provision or to privatization of infrastructure facilities. The fact that some PPPs are paid for by user fees leads us to the belief that PPPs are costless for government and should not be included in the fiscal balance sheet. However, when we consider their intertemporal effect on the budget, we are led to the conclusion that PPPs should be included in the fiscal balance sheet, so that their impact is the same as if they were part of the public sector. It follows that from a public finance perspective, PPPs are close to public provision. Without endemic contract renegotiation, however, the PPP mechanism provides incentives to be efficient and to reduce costs in the provision of infrastructure services. In this, a PPP resembles privatization in the incentives that are provided. However, in a fundamental sense, PPPs differ from privatization: contract length can be used to create risk-sharing arrangements that are not possible under privatization. In particular, it is possible to design flexible-term contracts, which can lead to large welfare gains.

Given the erroneous beliefs surrounding PPPs, what are their real benefits? First, the incentive to reduce life cycle costs fosters continuous maintenance, which is much cheaper than intermittent maintenance. This is especially valuable when quality of service is contractible, such as in highways. There are other reasons to expect better maintenance under PPPs. A PPP contract can specify that the infrastructure must be handed back in good condition at the end of the contract. This creates incentives for maintenance that are unavailable under public provision of an equivalent project.

Second, we believe that in a PPP project that collects user fees, users feel empowered to demand good service, and this requires continuous maintenance. When user fees are collected on a public infrastructure project, the perception is that funds will flow into the general budget or, at best, into a general infrastructure fund, so users feel less empowered.

Another potential advantage of PPPs is that when projects are fully funded by user fees and there is no space for opportunistic renegotiations, private firms will evaluate projects and discard those that are white elephants. In addition, the PPP will face fewer pressures to lower user fees than in the case of a publicly provided project, and this can lead to large increases in potential revenues from infrastructure projects. Finally, because revenue from user fees is received directly by the PPP, there is no distortion induced by general revenue taxes or by costs associated with the operation of the government bureaucracy required to disburse these funds to the private firm.

There are counterarguments in favor of public provision, not all of them convincing. Observed financing costs seem lower for the government than for private firms, but this is because governments can borrow to burn resources and the rate on government debt would not increase significantly – lenders look only at global indebtedness and do not evaluate individual public projects. Thus, the higher borrowing costs PPPs face are partly due to better project evaluation by lenders, and this is valuable. Furthermore, we argue that the higher borrowing costs of PPPs may be due to incorrect contract design, to the risk of regulatory takings and expropriations. Additionally, higher borrowing costs under PPPs include the costs associated with the transfer of endogenous risks to prevent moral hazard and to strengthen incentives to cut costs, the provision of adequate service quality, and the monitoring of management. A more compelling argument in favor of publicly funded projects is that they appear in the public balance sheet, so they cannot be used to anticipate public spending away from the purview of Congress. Finally, although there is scope for opportunistic renegotiations during the construction phase of a public project, there is no possibility of opportunistic renegotiation afterward, one of the most important problems associated with PPPs.

The previous argument suggests that public provision should be preferred over PPPs in most less-developed countries. Institutional development plays a more substantial role under PPPs than under public provision because governments must refrain from regulatory takings or from expropriating the project once investments are sunk. Under a PPP the continuing relationship provides more scope for opportunism. This book therefore concentrates on middle-income and developed countries where the institutional setup is sufficiently developed.

Regarding PPPs and types of infrastructure, we argue that there is scope for potentially large welfare gains under PPPs in the case of highways, tunnels, and bridges, where quality can be contracted and verified. Moreover, contracts can be designed so as to adapt to changing conditions without much scope for opportunism by either party. Even though the case is less clear cut, we also conclude that PPPs are likely to be better than public provision for other types of transport infrastructure, such as airports. By contrast, most of the advantages of PPPs are either absent or more difficult to establish in the case of complex infrastructure projects, such as hospitals and schools.

We began working on PPPs almost 20 years ago, writing academic papers and advising governments and multilateral organizations. Two years ago we decided to write a book detailing the main lessons we have learned from this experience. We believe our key conclusions can help design government policy that leads to better infrastructure at lower cost. Our aim in this book is to distill the lessons that are relevant for policy makers and to combine real-world evidence with the underlying economic arguments. For this reason, this is a work of synthesis that draws heavily on the research of others. That said, this book is not an all-encompassing, neutral survey, and not everybody will agree with our conclusions.

Indeed, we have strong and opinionated views on some issues, and on others we believe the jury is still out. At the policy level, PPPs have turned into an ideological issue, with some commentators in favor because they limit the role of governments and with others in opposition for that same reason. In contrast, we have tried hard to let the evidence and economic analysis temper our biases. The reader can decide to what extent we have succeeded.

Acknowledgments

We would like to acknowledge the encouragement and feedback we received from Eduardo Bitrán, Antonio Estache, J. Luis Guasch, William Hogan, Michael Klein, Guillermo Perry, and Jean Tirole, especially in the initial stages of our research on PPPs. They played an important role in stimulating our work by posing questions that kept us thinking over the years.

Many colleagues provided generous comments on chapters from the first draft of this book. We thank Claudio Agostini, Laure Athias, Thorsten Beckers, Germá Bel, Alonso Bucarey, Jose Carbajo, Mauricio Cárdenas, John Cheng, Ginés de Rus, Jean-Jacques Dethier, Antonio Estache, Katja Funke, Hugh Goldsmith, Andrés Gomez-Lobo, David Heald, William Hogan, Nicholas Hope, Elisabetta Iossa, Tim Irwin, Andreas Kappeler, Michael Klein, James Leigland, Benjamín Leiva, Lili Liu, Eduardo Lora, Marcela Meléndez, Richard Norment, Mike Parker, Guilermo Perry, Pierre Picard, Bob Poole, Mauricio Portugal, Isabel Rial, Ridwan Rusli, Pablo Sanguinetti, Stephane Saussier, Gerd Schwartz, Tomás Seribristky, Eytan Sheshinski, Chris Shugart, Robin Simpson, Kenneth Small, Nancy Smith, Stephane Straub, Shamsudin Tareq, Clemencia Torres, Timo Valila, Alan van der Hilst, Eric Verhoef, Xavier Vives, Felix Wagemann, Anthony Wall, Clifford Winston, E. R. Yescombe, and Richard Zeckhauser.

We gratefully acknowledge the generous financial support from the Corporación Andina de Fomento. Fischer and Galetovic thank the Instituto de Sistemas Complejos de Ingeniería for its support since 2005. Galetovic also thanks the Stanford Center for International Development and the Hoover Institution for their hospitality.

Thanks to Scott Parris and Karen Maloney at Cambridge University Press. And for outstanding help in editing the final version and composing the index, we are grateful to María Ignacia Varela.

It was not easy to avoid using equations throughout this book. For those readers who may be interested, we have written an appendix containing a bare bones model that formalizes in the simplest way possible many results that we mention in the text. Furthermore, we have avoided references whenever possible. Instead, we have included bibliographical notes at the end of each chapter, which acknowledge the main papers from which we have drawn. We have also drawn from our previous work, which appears in the following publications:

"The Basic Public Finance of Public Private Partnerships," *Journal of the European Economic Association* **11**, 83–111, 2013.

"The Economics of Infrastructure Finance: Public-Private Partnerships versus Public Provision," *EIB Studies* **15**, 40–69, 2010.

"Highway Franchising in the United States," *Review of Industrial Organization* **29**, 27–53, 2006.

"Highway Franchising and Real-Estate Values," *Journal of Urban Economics* **57**, 432–448, 2005.

"Privatizing Highways in Latin America: Fixing What Went Wrong," *Economia, The Journal of Lacea* **4**, 129–164, 2003.

"Least Present Value of Revenue Auctions and Highway Franchising," *Journal of Political Economy* **109**, 993–1020, 2001.

"Highway Franchising: Pitfalls and Opportunities," *American Economic Review* **87**, 68–72, 1997 (reprinted in *The Economics of Public Private Partnerships*, D. Grimsey and M. Lewis (eds.), Northampton: Edward Elgar, 2005).

1

Introduction

One of the main tasks of government is to provide infrastructure services at a reasonable cost. Infrastructure projects, such as highways, bridges, tunnels, and ports, are large, sunk investments that need to be maintained and operated once they are built. The process by which projects are selected, designed, operated, and maintained is therefore critical.

During the 1970s and 1980s, countries as diverse as the United Kingdom and Chile privatized many public enterprises, driven by both efficiency and ideological considerations. Public services such as telecommunications, electricity, and sanitation came first. Next, governments sought to extend the benefits of private participation to sectors deemed exceedingly difficult to privatize, such as transportation, schools, and hospitals. This led to the development of public-private partnerships (PPPs), long-term contracts between the state and a private company to provide infrastructure. These contracts bundle financing, construction, operation, and maintenance within a single firm.

Prior to PPPs, the state usually provided infrastructure. The construction of a project was contracted out to a private company and financed with taxes or public debt. The firm built the project and received the agreed payment, thereby completing the contract. Afterwards, a different division of government took charge of operating and maintaining the facility.

The separation between building and operating the project under public provision means that the design phase does not appropriately incorporate future maintenance and operating costs. Moreover, governments often prefer to spend resources on new projects rather than on routine maintenance. Lack of attention to maintenance leads to the decay of facilities and a deterioration of quality of service until governments respond to local pressures and rebuild or retrofit the infrastructure at high cost.

The use of PPPs introduced a new approach whereby a single private company finances and builds the project and is then responsible for the operation and maintenance of the installations, subject to performance standards.

PPPs have grown rapidly over the past two decades. Given the budgetary problems that many developed countries have faced since the 2008 financial crisis, this trend will most likely continue as those economies recover. The provision of infrastructure under the PPP model has been used in large projects such as highways, water and wastewater plants, power stations, bridges, seaports, airports, hospitals, jails, and schools. This trend and the experience of the past 25 years raise the questions this book seeks to answer: When should a PPP be preferred over public provision or privatization? How should PPPs be implemented? And what is the best governance structure for PPP contracts?

1.1 The Scope of This Book

Some Definitions

There are many definitions and types of infrastructure. For our purposes, *public infrastructure* refers to a long-lasting and irreversible investment used to provide public services, such as highways, seaports, airports, sanitation systems, schools, or hospitals. The variety of definitions of PPP that academics and practitioners use led Donahue and Zeckhauser to conclude that "the public-private association has become a perniciously broad category" (2011, p. 259). Nonetheless, most definitions include the participation of both the public and private sectors and the fact that the contract establishes how risk is shared between the two parties.

In this book, a PPP is defined as an agreement by which the government contracts a private company to build or improve infrastructure works and to subsequently maintain and operate them for an extended period (for example, 30 years) in exchange for a stream of revenues during the life of the contract. Sometimes, as in the case of a toll road, revenues accrue mainly from user fees. In other cases, as with hospitals, users are not charged and the government makes periodic payments. More generally, the concessionaire is remunerated with a combination of user fees and government transfers. In all cases, at the end of the contract the asset reverts to government control.

Public Provision, PPPs, and Privatization

There are three ways to provide infrastructure: public provision, PPPs, and privatization. Under public provision, a private firm builds the project, receives the negotiated payment, and concludes its contractual agreement with the government. In contrast, the company that builds or improves the infrastructure under a PPP also operates and maintains the project after the construction phase is completed. Privatization differs from a PPP in that the infrastructure is permanently transferred to the private company, and from that point on, the firm assumes all the associated business risks.[1]

In theory, under a PPP, the concessionaire assumes the risk of changes in maintenance and operating costs, unforeseen changes in revenues, and even the possibility of expropriation during the life of the contract. In practice, however, the contracts are ambiguous, and governments often share these risks while the contract is in force because of contract renegotiation.

The Scope of PPPs

While the issues addressed in this book are relevant for the majority of PPPs, one of our objectives is to delimit the type of infrastructure for which PPPs are appropriate and those for which traditional provision or privatization would be a better choice. The answer depends, in part, on the technical and economic characteristics of the infrastructure in question. Consequently, as discussed in Chapter 4, we have more to say about highways, where PPPs are especially suitable, than power stations, which generally work better under privatization, or schools, where PPPs are not a good choice because it is difficult to define objective performance standards.

Similarly, institutional development plays a more important role under PPPs than under public provision because the long-lived contractual relationship between the government and the concessionaire under a PPP provides more scope for expropriation and regulatory taking by the government.

[1] Each approach includes a range of contractual agreements. Guasch (2004) identifies 12 contractual forms that he organizes by increasing order of private participation: public supply and operation; outsourcing, corporatization, and performance agreements; management contract; leasing; franchise; concession; build-operate-transfer (BOT); build-own-operate; divestiture by license; divesture by sale; and private supply and operation. In this list, PPPs are represented by franchises, concessions, and BOT arrangements. Whether a lease (also known as an *affermage*) is a PPP depends on the definition used: for example, Guasch (2004) classifies it as a PPP, but Yescombe (2007) does not. In this book, we use the terms *PPP, concession,* and *franchise* interchangeably.

This explains why we concentrate on middle-income and developed countries, which tend to have institutions that work reasonably well or that can conceivably be improved, and less on low-income countries, where public provision is likely to suffer relatively less from the lack of a basic institutional framework than PPPs.

1.2 Trends

Figure 1.1 shows annual investment in PPPs in Europe from 1990 to 2011, both as actual values and as three-year centered moving averages. PPPs in Europe increased more than fivefold, on an annual basis, between the 1990s and 2005–2007. By contrast, investment in PPPs during 2009–2011 was 38 percent lower than during 2005–2007.

Table 1.1 shows investment in PPPs by country. PPPs account for the largest fraction of overall public investment in the United Kingdom and Portugal (27 percent and 21 percent, respectively, for the period between 2000 and 2009).[2] They have been used in Europe to award projects in defense, environmental protection, government buildings, hospitals, information technology, municipal services, prisons, recreation, schools, solid waste, transport (including airports, bridges, ports, rail, roads, tunnels, and urban railways), tourism, and water. The transport sector is the sector with the most investments in PPPs, accounting for 83 percent of PPP investments in Continental Europe and 36 percent in the United Kingdom. Two-thirds of the investment in the transport sector has been in roads. Table 1.2 shows the distribution of revenue sources for European PPPs for roads, bridges, and tunnels. For 61 percent of these projects, the main revenue source for the concessionaire is tolls paid by users, while tolls paid by the government, often referred to as *shadow tolls*, are the main source of compensation for 33 percent of projects. The remaining 6 percent correspond to availability contracts, where the government pays the concessionaire based on performance standards.

Figure 1.2 shows investment in PPPs in low- and middle-income countries. Investment grew at an average annual rate of 28.3 percent between 1990 and 1997, followed by a slowdown after the East Asian crisis. A new growth spurt began in 2003, with investment reaching $180 billion (U.S. billion) in 2010. In contrast with Europe, the impact of the financial crisis of 2009 barely affected the upward trend in PPPs in middle- and low-income countries.

---

[2] Other advanced economies with significant PPP programs include Australia, the Czech Republic, and Hungary (see Hemming, 2004).

Table 1.1. *PPP investment in Europe*

Country	Total investment, 1990–2006 (million €)	Fraction of public investment, 2001–6 (%)
Belgium	2,112	3.5
France	7,670	1.3
Germany	5,658	1.5
Greece	7,600	5.9
Hungary	5,294	7.3
Italy	7,269	2.5
Netherlands	3,339	2.2
Portugal	11,254	22.8
Spain	24,886	6.9
United Kingdom	112,429	32.5[a]

Source: Blanc-Brude, Goldsmith, and Välilä (2007).
Notes: The table lists the ten countries in Europe with the most investment.
a. If the London Underground is excluded, this becomes 20%.

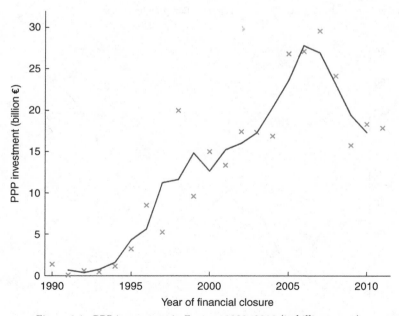

Figure 1.1. PPP investment in Europe, 1990–2011 (in billion euros).

Table 1.2. *Toll type for PPP roads, bridges, and tunnels in Europe, 1990–2007*

	(1) Availability contract	(2) Real toll	(3) Shadow toll	(4) Total
Austria	0	2	0	2
Finland	2	0	0	2
France	0	8	0	8
Germany	0	8	0	8
Greece	0	6	0	6
Hungary	0	5	0	5
Ireland	0	8	0	8
Italy	0	7	0	7
Latvia	1	0	0	1
Netherlands	2	0	1	3
Norway	0	3	0	3
Poland	0	1	1	2
Portugal	0	6	11	17
Spain	0	31	14	45
United Kingdom	4	3	20	27
Total	9	88	47	144

Source: Data kindly provided by Timo Välilä at the European Investment Bank.

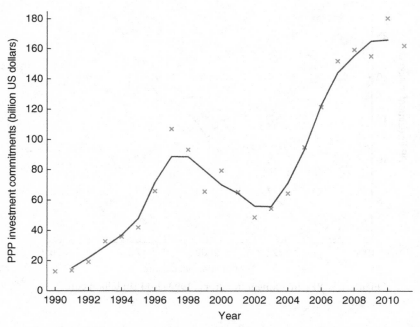

Figure 1.2. PPP investment in low- and middle-income countries, 1990–2011 (in million U.S. dollars).

Table 1.3. *PPP investment in developing countries, 1990–2008*

Country	Energy[a]	Telecommunications[a]	Transport	Water and sewage	Total
	U.S. dollars				
Argentina	29,540	29,328	14,094	8,176	81,137
Brazil	75,993	107,554	32,142	4,576	220,265
China	37,339	14,518	47,449	8,427	107,732
India	45,868	52,898	24,766	331	123,864
Indonesia	15,492	24,972	3,743	1,020	45,228
Malaysia	14,313	9,596	16,552	10,144	50,605
Mexico	10,753	54,068	25,374	1,675	91,869
Philippines	19,268	14,280	3,478	8,071	45,096
Russia	30,484	48,813	706	2,225	82,228
Turkey	12,678	24,293	8,170	942	46,082

Source: World Bank-PPIAF PPI database.
Notes: The table lists the 10 developing countries with the most investment.
a. Projects in this sector do not fit our definition for PPPs, because they correspond to infrastructure that is privatized and regulated as a natural monopoly.

Table 1.3 presents detailed information for the 10 developing countries that have invested most via PPPs and covers the energy, telecommunications, transport, and water sectors. Most projects in energy and telecommunications are regulated utilities and, given the perspective on PPPs that we adopt in this book, are better classified under private provision.

Although the United States lags behind Europe and many developing countries in the use of PPPs, its growth rates have been impressive. Figure 1.3 shows PPP investments in the U.S. transport sector during the past two decades (no reliable data are available for other sectors). Investment via PPPs increased almost fivefold, on an annual basis, between the decade of 1998–2007 and the three-year period of 2008–2010. Approximately $23 billion was invested in this sector via PPPs between 1998 and 2011.

The evidence presented in this section suggests that PPPs are becoming an increasingly important mechanism for the provision of infrastructure in Europe, developing countries, and the United States. In the next three sections, we explore the extent to which PPPs live up to the expectations that were created 30 years ago, when the current wave of PPPs began. We begin with a brief diagnostic of the shortcomings of public provision. Next we examine the various arguments used to make the case that PPPs effectively address these issues. Finally, we assess the major shortcomings of PPPs in dealing with these problems.

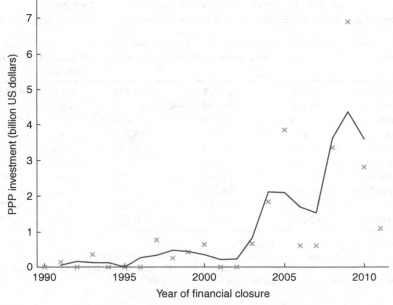

Figure 1.3. Growth of PPP investment in the U.S. transport sector, 1990–2011
(in million U.S. dollars).

1.3 Problems with Public Provision

Governments face four challenges when providing infrastructure services: First, choosing which projects should be built – that is, government must have a plan and a procedure for selecting projects; second, verifying that built projects fulfill their service obligations – this is more exacting than having the project comply with a set of technical requirements; and third, ensuring that neither the government nor the public are overcharged in a fee-for-service model. The fourth challenge is to finance the infrastructure, which requires finding the necessary resources, either from the government's budget or through user fees.

Infrastructure is a sector in which governments usually fail to meet these objectives. For example, although 6,000 kilometers of new roads were paved in Brazil between 1979 and 1984, 8,000 kilometers of old roads deteriorated because of poor-quality maintenance, so the stock of fair- to good-quality roads decreased (see Rioja, 2003). Some of the reasons for this failure are political and organizational; others relate to specific aspects of infrastructure provision. The first group includes political capture, corruption, and bureaucratic deficiencies. The second involves technical difficulties and the inability to predict future demand trends or technical advances.

Poor Project Selection

Few countries use social project evaluation to filter wasteful projects. This leads to projects that are white elephants (that is, projects that have negative social value or that are overengineered). Even when objective criteria for project evaluation exist, they may be distorted by underestimating costs and overestimating demand, two common problems of infrastructure provision.[3]

One of the reasons for poor project selection is the capture of government objectives in the interest of only a subgroup of society. This distortion may steer project choices away from those that benefit society at large or lead to projects that are too expensive but benefit specific lobbies. Pork-barrel politics is an example of capture of government: the political establishment, seeking reelection, pressures government into building new projects for its constituencies, independent of the efficient assignment of resources. This leads to underutilized projects, such as bridges to nowhere in Alaska and other places.[4]

An example of a country with numerous white elephants is Belgium, where the political pressures to replicate spending on both sides of the linguistic divide led to a category of projects denominated *grands travaux inútils*. These include several kilometers of abandoned subway tunnels, almost-empty light rail lines, and many unused viaducts and bridges.[5]

Infrastructure Maintenance

The incentives politicians face distract them from assigning resources for routine maintenance. Building new projects and reconstructing severely damaged infrastructure are more effective uses of resources from the political viewpoint, so maintenance spending often goes only to severely impaired infrastructure. The cost of this stop-and-go approach is much higher than the cost of continuous maintenance – a tripling of costs is common in the case of roads. Moreover, while the road is in disrepair, which occurs during

---

[3] See Flyvbjerg, Holm, and Buhl (2002, 2005) for extensive evidences.
[4] Cadot, Röller, and Stephan (2006) show that pork barrel is an important determinant of transport infrastructure choices in France.
[5] See *Le Petit Guide des Grands Travaux Inutiles*, Jean-Claude Defossé (1990).

a substantial fraction of its life, speeds are lower and vehicles using the road are damaged (see Chapter 3). Finally, the increased risk of accidents is an additional cost of inadequate maintenance.

Inefficient Pricing
Under public provision, user fees are usually set too low for political reasons. This is inefficient because it may lead to congestion of the facility, overuse of the service, or lack of maintenance because user fees do not even cover variable costs. In addition, the distributional impact is negative because the heaviest users are usually the wealthiest segment of the population, or because the poorest segments are excluded from the service.

Capture and Corruption
Another problem is sectorial capture of government by the construction lobby, caused by repeated interaction between a few large construction firms and government. In particular, firms may try to use their influence to limit competition, for instance, by requiring qualifications that exclude newcomers or foreign firms. For example, the PPP law passed in Brazil in 2004 included conditions that precluded the participation of foreign firms in PPPs involving the transport sector.[6] The construction lobby may also use the political system to put pressure on the government in return for campaign donations. It may threaten to stop participation in new projects in response to attempts to improve the oversight of the infrastructure procurement process. Similarly, attempts at stringent supervision may lead to strategic delays in finishing the project, with the associated political cost. Alternatively, politicians may push for early completion of a project, even if this means that the terms of the contract have to be renegotiated at a high cost after the election.

Finally, there may be outright corruption, in which the government favors certain projects and firms, accepts the influence of specific firms in the design of contracts, or allows modification (renegotiation) of the terms of a contract to favor a firm in response to direct or indirect hidden payments.

---

[6] In the first years after the 2004 law was introduced, capital and other financial requirements were used as an exclusionary mechanism against foreign firms because their leverage was higher than the norm in Brazil. See Portugal (2010, pp. 36–37).

Poor Institutional Design

In what follows, we lump the government agencies in charge of infrastructure provision into the public works authority (PWA). The PWA is responsible for investing vast resources and has a wider scope for discretionary action than departments of government in which most of the expenditure is destined to pay for personnel, such as the armed forces, education, and health. This makes it particularly important to check the PWA's capacity for undertaking discretionary action.

Unfortunately, the institutional design of the PWA is deficient in many countries. There is no independent supervisory authority that approves projects, enforces contracts, and oversees the quality of construction, maintenance, and services. If these functions are performed at all, they are assigned to a separate internal division within the PWA. Worse still, these supervisory functions are sometimes located within the procurement division itself, eliminating any capacity for efficient and independent supervision. The strategic planning division of the PWA frequently lacks authority and independence, so it tends to respond to short-term political objectives.

In sum, the poor institutional design of the PWA in most countries exacerbates agency problems, resulting in the selection of the wrong projects for construction, the payment of excessive costs for infrastructure services, and poor maintenance of existing infrastructure.

Renegotiation

An environment in which contract renegotiations are common tends to dissuade firms that are technically efficient but lack lobbying ability because they may be unable to compete with inefficient firms that are good at lobbying. Stricter enforcement of contracts may induce the entry of more efficient firms in the long run, but this benefit is of little use for a politician seeking reelection. Consequently, public works often suffer from cost overruns and delays, which is a form of contract renegotiation. Even when construction contracts specify that bonds must be posted to ensure that deadlines are met and quality standards are satisfied, these are frequently not collected when contractual conditions are not satisfied.

1.4 Promises

Advocates of PPPs have offered many arguments to show that PPPs may help governments provide infrastructure more efficiently. A common claim is that PPPs relieve budgetary restrictions and release public funds. For instance, the *Financial Times* has claimed, "The boom [in PPPs] is good news for governments with overstretched public finances: many local and national authorities have found themselves sitting on toll roads, ports, and airports that they can sell for billions of dollars to fund other public services."[7]

A second argument is that because financing of the project is private, it is subject to the discipline of the financial market, which leads to important efficiency gains. A third claim is that PPPs lead to efficiency gains because they bundle construction with operation and maintenance. A fourth argument is that PPPs can mimic a competitive market because they are often adjudicated in competitive auctions. Fifth, even though user fees can be charged under both public provision and PPPs, the fact that there is at least one party interested in setting profitable tolls under PPPs balances the political pressures to lower fees. Sixth, PPPs should help filter white elephants. Lastly, various arguments have been given to justify PPPs on distributional grounds.[8]

Relieving Government Budgets
Governments often argue that PPPs free up scarce government resources for use in programs that are socially attractive but not privately profitable. Similarly, PPPs allow governments to provide the infrastructure without raising taxes. This argument obviously does not apply to PPPs whose capital costs are funded by future government payments using contracts that specify a schedule of capital charges payable in the future and that thus bind the intertemporal budget. In these cases, PPPs help governments perform a useful accounting trick in which future obligations are kept off the balance sheet for no clear economic reason. For example, the United Kingdom, a major user of this type of PPP, has discovered that the capital charges for past investments are constraining the current budget of local authorities.

The argument that PPPs can relieve tight government budgets is doubtful even for projects whose capital costs are partially or totally covered by user fees. In this case, user fees could have been used to pay the capital costs under public provision as well. The resources that the government saved by not paying the upfront investment under a PPP should be equal, in present value, to user-fee revenue foregone to the concessionaire. That is, from a financial viewpoint, PPPs borrow from the future with no net gain in discounted terms.

---

[7] "Route to reward," *Financial Times*, July 5, 2007. p. 7.
[8] In addition, when there is political opposition to privatization, a PPP can be more palatable because the facilities eventually return to the government.

Is there an exception to this argument when a government is credit constrained but expects to be less so in the future? Does a PPP on a self-financing road increase the resources available to the credit-constrained government? To answer this question, note again that the government could have built the project and collected user fees, obtaining exactly the same discounted revenue as with the PPP. Therefore, the credit-constrained government could have asked for a loan against these funds. It is probable that lenders would ask the government to set aside the toll revenue in a special trust fund kept isolated from general government revenues. If the institutional conditions in the country do not provide an effective separation between the trust fund and general revenues, thus allowing the government the opportunity to divert the funds to the general budget, lenders would anticipate this and the country would remain credit constrained. Thus, PPPs do not increase the access to international loans for public infrastructure investment.

We conclude that governments often choose PPPs because they allow them to make public investments while keeping future obligations off the balance sheet and beyond legislative control. This is not a valid economic justification for PPPs.

Efficiency Gains

A standard argument in favor of privatization is that private firms are more efficient than state-owned enterprises. This argument does not apply directly to the construction phase when comparing PPPs to public provision because governments rely on private firms to build, maintain, and operate infrastructure under both organizational forms. Furthermore, the firms responsible for construction are often the same under public provision and PPPs. This suggests that any argument linking PPPs with efficiency gains has to be subtler.

The academic literature emphasizes the importance of bundling construction and maintenance as a source of efficiency gains. With public provision, a construction firm minimizes building costs subject to design characteristics. In a PPP, by contrast, the private firm minimizes life-cycle costs, which include building, operating, and maintenance costs, even if this leads to higher initial construction costs. As argued in Chapter 4, when the quality of service is contractible, PPPs are preferable to traditional provision because the concessionaire internalizes life-cycle costs during the building phase without compromising service quality. To the extent that investments during the building phase can lower maintenance and operating costs, this should lead to efficiency gains under PPPs. This potential advantage of bundling is even greater under privatization because in this case the firm owns the asset indefinitely. However, this option is often ruled out because having the infrastructure return periodically to government ownership facilitates long-term network planning.

We are not aware of studies illustrating the quantitative importance of bundling. The efficiency gains are probably large, however, given the interaction of bundling with the political economy of infrastructure provision. Under public provision, most governments spend too little on routine maintenance and too much on new projects or on major reconstruction of existing projects because it is more attractive for politicians to inaugurate new projects than to do routine maintenance on existing facilities. By contrast, under a PPP that specifies and enforces quality standards, maintaining the infrastructure adequately is usually optimal for the concessionaire. PPPs thus create more incentives to provide adequate maintenance than traditional provision.

There is also anecdotal evidence that PPPs can lower construction and operating costs. For example, the concessionaire that built express lanes on State Route 91 in Orange County, California, reduced construction time substantially by using innovations in traffic management during construction.[9] In France, moving from public provision of highways to PPPs during the 1980s seems to have substantially reduced the cost of construction (Gómez-Ibañez and Meyer, 1993, p. 201). PPPs provide strong incentives to finish the project early because profits increase when users can be charged at an earlier date. Incentives of this sort are usually absent (or considerably weaker) under traditional provision.

Introducing Competition

In many countries, the rates that public providers, such as utilities, charge are often so low that they lead to overconsumption and underinvestment. When utilities are privatized, rates increase (in some cases leading to protests and renationalization, as with the water works in El Alto, Bolivia), but investment also rises. This combination generates an improvement in the quality of service and a reduction of wasteful consumption. Setting user fees too low has contributed to macroeconomic instability in several developing countries in the not-so-distant past.

When infrastructure is privatized, there is a similar risk that user fees may be set too low as a result of regulatory takings in response to political

---

[9] See Small (2010). We describe this project in Chapter 3.

pressures. There is also the opposite risk: user fees may be set at a level that leads to excessive profits, reflecting regulatory capture. A vast literature addresses these problems.

PPPs could result in fees that are closer to efficient pricing because they do not depend on the government and are somewhat insulated from political pressure by their explicit contractual arrangement. In that case, an alternative to tariff setting by an imperfect regulator is a competitive process for price determination. Long ago, Chadwick (1859) argued that PPPs can avoid these regulatory difficulties if the firm is chosen via a competitive auction, where the bidding variable is the user fee (see also Demsetz, 1968). In Chadwick's terms, competition *for* the field is a close substitute for competition *in* the field, leading to the efficient price and eliminating economic rents for the service provider.

The benefits of so-called Demsetz auctions can only materialize if there is real competition for the contract. This is often not the case. In some countries (Brazil is an example), the PPP legislation biases auctions in favor of domestic participants, for example, by demanding documentation that is only available to domestic firms. In other cases (such as Colombia and Argentina in recent years), the government's overt or covert objective is to spread the projects among the main domestic construction firms. Because these practices decrease competition, the cost of infrastructure rises and the quality may be reduced. Nevertheless, the most important limitation of Demsetz auctions when applied to PPPs comes from the pervasive use of renegotiations, a topic we consider shortly.

Charging Appropriate User Fees
Under public provision of infrastructure services, user fees might be too low in response to political considerations (see the case of the Chicago Skyway in Section 2.3). Organizations can wield more power than individual voters, so groups with effective lobbying power, such as truckers in the case of highways, are often able to negotiate fees that are below the marginal cost of their contribution to increased costs from wear and tear. Road wear and tear is proportional – as a rule of thumb – to a number between the third and fourth power of axle weight (see Small, Winston, and Evans, 1989, p. 11).

This indicates that in most countries, the tolls truck drivers pay are much lower than the wear-and-tear costs their trucks cause. There is no evidence, though, that PPPs have brought truck tolls close to the marginal cost the vehicles impose on road maintenance, given the power of organized truckers.

A potential advantage of PPPs is that they can lead to more efficient pricing. Nominal tolls on the Indiana Toll Road remained unchanged for more than 20 years under state ownership and management. In real terms, they fell substantially over this period. When the road was auctioned as a PPP in January 2006, tolls doubled and were indexed to inflation. The likely reason was that otherwise potential concessionaires would have overcharged initially to guard against the inflation risk over the long contract period (75 years). Indiana eventually yielded to the complaints of users, however, and lowered the tolls through 2016, compensating the concessionaire for the reduction at an estimated cost of $150 million (U.S. million). Other U.S. states, including Florida, Pennsylvania, and Texas, have since adopted toll indexation for their PPP projects.

As this example illustrates, PPPs can help governments avoid the temptation to charge inefficiently low user fees, while also ensuring adequate maintenance.

Filtering White Elephants

Adam Smith mentioned that when infrastructure is privately provided and sustained with user fees, a market test filters white elephants: "When high roads are ... made and supported by the commerce which is carried on by means of them, they can be made only where that commerce requires them."[10] This filter works only when PPPs are financed mainly with user fees because projects that are not expected to be profitable will fail to attract a concessionaire. However, financing capital expenses with user fees may lead to user charges that are higher than socially optimal, and this can be avoided under public provision. The large number of existing infrastructure projects that are white elephants suggests that the benefits of a market test that avoids projects that are overengineered (or outright unjustified) is likely to outweigh this social cost.[11]

Income Distribution

A frequent criticism of PPPs is their adverse distributional impact. For example, critics often argue that toll roads are unfair to lower-income users.

---

[10]   Adam Smith, *The Wealth of Nations* (1776), book 5, chapter 1, part 3, p. 1.
[11]   See Flyvbjerg, Holm, and Buhl (2002, 2005) for extensive evidence of overoptimistic demand and cost estimates in infrastructure projects.

This is an argument for rationing (by congestion) as opposed to a market solution. This argument loses force, however, in the case of greenfield projects, that is, projects that add to the stock of transport infrastructure. Lower-income users benefit from the existence of new toll roads in several ways. First, congestion is reduced when some users are diverted from the original roads to the tolled highways. Second, whenever there is an urgent need for rapid transportation, there is the option of paying for it, and this must be better than not having the option. Third, those who benefit most directly from the new highway pay for it, so the burden does not fall on taxpayers.

Leases, which involve a temporary transfer of property but no major improvements of the facility, are different from greenfield projects and cannot be justified on distributional grounds. User fees are usually allowed to rise after the lease contract is signed, so users pay more without enjoying the benefits of new infrastructure. An exception is when there are obvious operational improvements as could happen in the case of water and sewage. Brownfield projects that improve an existing infrastructure lie in between greenfield projects and leases in terms of their distributional impact. If the infrastructure was publicly provided and no user fees were charged prior to the brownfield project, users could end up worse off.

1.5 Practice

PPPs cannot exist in a country unless certain preconditions are met. Most important, there must be some certainty about the continued protection of property rights, including those arising from contracts with the PWA. Otherwise, private firms will not commit large upfront investments that will be paid by future revenue flows (such as user fees, shadow fees, and availability payments), or if they do, they will demand a prohibitively high premium to bear this risk. A well-developed financial market also helps because it allows firms to securitize the project locally after it is built, without paying large premiums to compensate for exchange rate uncertainty and country risk. PPPs are not an option when property rights protection is weak, and the PWA should then strive to improve public provision for infrastructure provision (see Chapter 7). Alternatively, multilaterals might help circumvent these prerequisites in some countries.

Despite many reasonable claims in their favor, the experience with PPPs has been mixed. In some cases, expectations were met, but in many other cases, contracts have been renegotiated (often in favor of the concessionaire) or been subject to regulatory takings. PPPs are also used to circumvent budgetary oversight and anticipate government spending because fiscal accounting standards for PPPs are primitive in most countries. In addition, the pervasive use of government revenue guarantees has reduced the potential of PPPs to filter white elephants. Despite the claims of efficiency, deadlines are not always met, or the projects require unplanned subsidies before they are finished and operated. Moreover, these subsidies are granted opaquely and without competition. This does not mean that public provision to infrastructure provision would do better.[12] As we argue throughout this book and especially in the summary in Chapter 9, if the right lessons are learned from recent experience, PPPs can become the correct organizational form for various types of infrastructure.

Well-Known Shortcomings

Some of the shortcomings of PPPs were known from the beginning of the current wave of private participation in infrastructure. For example, the high contracting costs associated with PPPs limit their use to sufficiently large projects and explain why many countries have a minimum investment requirement for PPPs (£20 million in the United Kingdom). Another well-known problem with PPPs is that when they are financed via user fees (and there is little or no congestion), these fees have to be set considerably above marginal cost so as to finance the upfront investment. The expectation is that the inefficiencies of second-best pricing will be offset by the many advantages associated with this option.

Governments and policy makers in the late 1980s and early 1990s largely overlooked two problems that became major issues: opportunistic renegotiations and the use of PPPs to circumvent budgetary controls.

Renegotiations

As Williamson (1976, 1985) pointed out, the problem with Demsetz auctions is that the competitive process takes place when the concessionaire is selected. During the remainder of the long-term contract that characterizes a PPP, the relationship between the government and the concessionaire is a bilateral monopoly, which creates hold-up opportunities. First, because the investment is sunk and the firm cannot vote with its feet, the government can be opportunistic and there is scope for regulatory takings.

---

[12] For an early evaluation of infrastructure PPPs, see EPAC (1995). For more recent evaluations, see Engel, Fischer, and Galetovic (2004) and Grimsey and Lewis (2007).

Second, given the technical, legal, and political difficulties of taking over the project without major market disruptions, it is difficult to punish the firm for noncompliance. This means the firm has some leeway, and therefore incentives, to behave opportunistically – for instance, by lowering service quality.

In a bilateral monopoly, both sides can try to renegotiate the original contract. There is strong evidence that this has occurred with PPPs. Guasch (2004) studies a sample of more than 1,000 infrastructure concessions awarded in Latin America between 1985 and 2000. He finds that more than half of the original contracts were changed substantially (54.7 percent in the transport sector; 74.4 percent in the water sector) and that the average time between adjudication and the first renegotiation of the contract was slightly more than three years. Moreover, most renegotiation processes were initiated by the firms. Earlier evidence from PPPs in the transport sector, in both industrialized and middle-income countries, suggests that concessionaires are generally bailed out by governments when they run into financial trouble, which happens often (Gómez-Ibañez and Meyer, 1993).

The prevalence of opportunistic renegotiations overturns many of the potential advantages of PPPs. If firms can renegotiate contracts to obtain additional government transfers when they have losses, then PPPs will not help avoid white elephants. Incentives to filter white elephants have been blunted even further by government guarantees, such as the so-called minimum income guarantees.

Another problem associated with opportunistic renegotiations is that selecting the concessionaire in a competitive auction is less beneficial than the literature on Demsetz auctions suggests. The selected firms will be biased toward lobbying and renegotiation rather than technical expertise.[13] The explanation is that firms that survive in the long run cannot be relatively worse in both dimensions (renegotiation and technical ability) because firms that are better in both dimensions would outperform them. Hence, there is a frontier of surviving firms, in which better lobbying and renegotiating ability is associated with poorer technical competence. Thus, firms that are better in the technical dimension will be at a disadvantage in countries with a higher propensity to renegotiate contracts (which will attract firms that are better at lobbying), and they will gravitate to other countries.

---

[13] See Engel, Fischer, and Galetovic (2008) for a formal analysis.

Soft Budgets

An important type of government failure is caused by the tendency of governments, prompted by the election cycle, to heavily discount the future. As mentioned earlier, governments would like to anticipate infrastructure spending in the expectation of increasing their chances of reelection. Anticipating infrastructure expenditures under public provision is complicated by budgetary controls (such as congressional approval) that limit the government's ability to impose liabilities on future administrations. By contrast, selling state-owned assets allows the current administration to spend with little oversight, as in the case of the Chicago Skyway. PPPs have also been used extensively to anticipate government spending. First, PPPs do not contribute to the national debt because fiscal accounting rules in most countries consider them to be off the balance sheet. This led the *Economist* to explain the U.K. government's enthusiasm for the PPP program (called the Private Finance Initiative, or PFI, see Section 2.1) as follows: "Cynics suspect that the government remains keen on PFI not because of the efficiencies it allegedly offers, but because it allows ministers to perform a useful accounting trick."[14]

Long-term obligations derived from PPP contracts, such as government guarantees, often do not figure in the public accounts. Furthermore, PPPs often allow governments to finance new projects, unrelated to the original project, while avoiding budgetary controls. For example, in 2001 there was extensive flooding in Santiago, Chile, which led to political pressures on the government to invest in main collectors that would drain the rainwater from flood-prone areas. Because the government was unwilling to obtain funding from the budget or issue debt, it decided to renegotiate the PPP contracts for the urban highways to include building the drains. The drains added several hundred million dollars to the highway project and required the renegotiation of three major urban concession contracts. The initial payments for the additional works were scheduled to begin several years in the future.

1.6 Book Outline

We have set the stage for the main questions this book seeks to answer. To motivate the analysis in the rest of this book, Chapters 2 and 3 examine PPPs in practice. Chapter 2 describes PPP programs in the United Kingdom,

---

[14] "Singing the blues: Recession is heaping problems on a controversial form of public investment," *The Economist*, July 2, 2009.

Chile, the United States, and China. While each study highlights a different problem, the four cases taken together suggest that the shortcomings of PPP programs are similar across countries and stem from a combination of poor incentives, defective accounting standards, and inadequate governance. Chapter 3 examines PPPs in a particular type of infrastructure – highways – to illustrate the economic and physical characteristics that are necessary for PPPs to be a better option than both public provision and privatization.

Chapters 4 to 6 put PPPs in context. When should PPPs be used? How should they be designed and implemented? How should governments account for them in the budget? Chapter 4 examines incentives in PPPs and sets out conditions under which PPPs are better than public provision or privatization. Chapter 5 studies private finance and explains why PPPs are amenable to project financing, a financial technique that helps to borrow against the cash flow of a project that is legally and economically self-contained. We also examine the so-called PPP premium – whether PPPs are inherently more expensive to finance than public projects – and conclude that arguments against PPPs based on this premium are overrated. Chapter 6 examines the place of PPPs in the public budget and in the balance sheet. It also assesses the common claim that PPPs relieve strained budgets and enlarge the set of projects that can be financed and undertaken.

Chapters 7 and 8 examine the main threats facing PPPs. Chapter 7 deals with pervasive renegotiations, which may render moot many of the potential advantages of PPPs. Chapter 8 explains why good governance is necessary for PPPs to work and argues that nowhere are these conditions satisfied even closely. It also sketches the design of an efficient governance structure in charge of planning and delivering infrastructure in general and PPPs in particular, and of monitoring contract compliance.

Finally, Chapter 9 summarizes the lessons learned, and answers the questions of when PPPs are the best choice and how PPP contracts and governance should be implemented. Several of these proposals have been recently incorporated into the PPP legislation in a number of countries.

Last, we include an appendix with a simple model that formalizes many of the insights underlying the main arguments in this book.

Bibliographic Notes

The best-known general introduction to PPPs is Grimsey and Lewis (2004a). See also OECD (2008). Shorter introductions are de Bettignies and

Ross (2004), Hemming (2006), IMF (2004), and Sadka (2006). Grimsey and
Lewis (2005b) collect many articles on PPPs. Vaillancourt-Rosenau (2000)
and Akintoye, Beck, and Hardcastle (2003) are useful collections of essays.
Estache (2006) takes stock of the experience with PPPs.

2

Country Studies

In this chapter, we analyze the experience of four countries that have used PPPs extensively: the United Kingdom, Chile, the United States, and China. Each case highlights one of the shortcomings that have plagued PPPs around the world. Britain's Public Finance Initiative shows how a PPP program can be used to sidestep budgetary limits by using off-balance-sheet finance. Chile's concession program illustrates how pervasive renegotiations can put in doubt the legitimacy of a relatively successful PPP program. PPPs in the United States show how they can be used to anticipate spending. Finally, China's vast PPP program in infrastructure exemplifies, by defect, the importance of the rule of law and institutions for the sustainability of PPPs. Our analysis sets out the basic principles of each PPP program, describing its history and scope and providing a general evaluation of the programs. The purpose of this chapter is to illustrate the shortcomings of PPPs, setting the stage for the conceptual analysis in the chapters that follow.

2.1 United Kingdom

The Private Finance Initiative (PFI) has become an important part of public investment in the United Kingdom. As of March 2011, the total estimated capital value of PFI projects across the United Kingdom was £52.8 billion.[1] By March 2011, 698 projects had reached financial close with 630 projects in operation. They include projects in transport, education,

---

[1] These data are from H. M. Treasury workbook, PFI signed projects list, March 2011. According to Harrison (2007), investment via PFI represented 11 percent of total U.K. public sector investment between 1998 and 2004. The Treasury data includes all projects that had reached financial close by March 16, 2011. These data do not include PPPs that predate the Private Finance Initiative introduced in the Autumn Statement of 1992 by the Chancellor of the Exchequer.

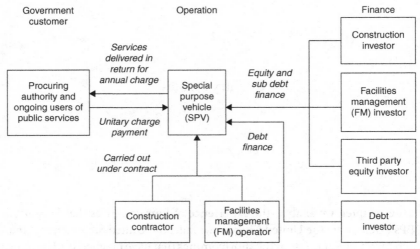

Figure 2.1. Structure of a PFI project.

health, prisons, defense, leisure, housing, courts, technology, and government offices. Twenty percent of spending was made in health, 25 percent in transport, 15 percent in education, and 15 percent in defense, with the remaining 25 percent distributed among projects in other areas. The future government obligations associated with this investment amount to £239 billion, with a present value, discounted at an annual rate of 3.5 percent, of £165 billion. This last sum includes not only the capital payments, but also the cleaning, catering, and maintenance expenses (the latter are referred to as *operating expenses* or "opex") associated with running these assets (H. M. Treasury, 2011).

The basic structure of a project is described in Figure 2.1. At its center stands a special purpose vehicle (SPV), which contracts with the procuring authority to provide public services. The SPV is usually formed by an equity investor, which provides 5–20 percent of the funding, a facilities management investor, and a construction investor. Senior debt provides the remaining funding. The objective of this funding structure is to provide due diligence for the project. The SPV hires a construction contractor and a facilities management provider (which can be the partners in the SPV) to build the project and provide the services. In exchange, the procuring authority pays an annual unitary charge.

A 2008 evaluation by an accounting firm shows that senior debt is providing due diligence services, and that the process has led to some financial discipline in the procurement authority and in the risk allocation methodology they use (PwC, 2008). This report recognizes, however, that the financing role by itself has no social value in a country with no government borrowing restrictions, a topic we discuss in Chapter 5. Senior debt has, thus far, recorded only limited losses when projects fail, but the equity provider has lost substantial amounts on failed projects, as in the case of the Dudley Group of Hospitals, Jarvis PLC in educational projects, and the National Physical Laboratory.

The importance of appropriate incentives is illustrated by the London Underground Metronet PFI that went bankrupt because of cost overruns in 2007. According to the House of Lords Select Committee on Economic Affairs (2010), this much-publicized bankruptcy gave PFI projects a bad name in the United Kingdom.[2] Uncertainty regarding whether Metronet would be able to borrow enough funds to finance the upgrade of the London Underground led Transport of London to guarantee 95 percent of its debt. This blunted the incentives for lenders to provide due diligence. The fact that the companies behind Metronet were allowed to have little of their equity at risk did not help either. So when the SPV failed, the central government had to step in to help the city of London meet its obligations by guaranteeing Metronet's debt. The National Accounting Office (NAO) estimates the direct loss to taxpayers to be somewhere between £170 million and £410 million.

As in most countries, the U.K. PPP program started slowly, with little standardization in procurement and contractual terms. Early projects, such as the Dartford Crossing and the Second Severn Crossing, inaugurated in 1991 and 1996, respectively, predate the PFI. These investments were governed by the Ryrie Rules, which required that the public budget be reduced by an amount equal to the sum of privately financed projects (House of Lords, 2010); our analysis in Section 6.1 justifies this requirement. This constraint was removed with the introduction of the Private Finance Initiative (PFI) by the Conservative Government in 1992. Use of the PFI did not become common until the Labor Government came to office in 1997. One reason was that the private sector was no longer required to bear demand risk (Connolly, Martin, and Wall, 2008).

In 2000, the government published a document that defined the PFI as "arrangements where the public sector contracts to purchase quality services on a long-term basis so as to take advantage of private sector management skills incentivised by having private finance at risk" (H. M. Treasury,

---

[2]   Gómez-Ibáñez (2007) identifies high-profile failures as a major reason for the discredit of PPPs in many countries.

2003). In this definition, PFI is different from introducing private sector ownership into state-owned businesses or selling government services using private sector expertise and finance.

In the government approach to PFI, three principles stand out (H. M. Treasury, 2003). First, the public sector specifies the outputs it requires from the private counterparties. Second, parties share the risk, with each party managing the risks it is best able to control. Risk assignment was a key element in evaluations of PFI projects in the 2003 Treasury report. For example, the SPV is responsible for delays in construction and service quality. Third, the public sector ensures the quality and continued effective delivery of public services. It has the power to reduce payments for poor performance, the flexibility to make necessary changes in the future, and the right to terminate the contract.

According to the 2003 Treasury report, many of the benefits of PFI are derived from the assignment of risk: desired standards are maintained for fear of penalties or possible cancellation of the contract; the project is more likely to be operational on time because the operator does not receive payment until services are provided; there is less risk of cost overruns (more about this later); and the design should minimize maintenance and operating costs over the lifetime of the project.

The basic principle in the PFI approach is that PPPs are only used when they offer value for money (VFM), defined as "the optimum combination of whole-life cost and quality (or fitness for purpose) to meet the user requirement" (Office of Government Commerce, 2002). The implementation of this principle involves a number of procedures over and above an assessment of the basic cost: the use of a least-cost solution that includes the maintenance of quality standards and the permanence of the PFI contractor; consideration of the terms and conditions imposed on workers the project transfers or employs; and a full evaluation of costs and benefits over the life cycle (including risks). The contract for the project does not specify inputs, but rather the required outputs, as well as the basis for payment of the services if the performance standards are satisfied. To implement the VFM approach, the methodology requires the existence of a public sector comparator (PSC), which corresponds to the estimated cost of providing "alternative services managed by the public sector and assuming the use of public sector capital investment" (H. M. Treasury, 1999).

The United Kingdom began to publicize the future budgetary disbursements of PFI projects early on. Yet under the accounting conventions used until 2009, most PFI deals were classified as off-balance sheet, and despite the more stringent accounting standards introduced in April 2009, PFI projects remain excluded from public sector net debt calculations (NAO, 2011).

Evaluation

In 2002, the Treasury conducted a sample study of 61 projects, out of 451 projects operational at the time (H. M. Treasury, 2003). The conclusions were positive. First, the percentage of projects that were late was much lower than under public provision, in studies by both the NAO and the Treasury (12 percent were late under PFI compared with 30 percent under public provision according to the latter study).[3] Under PFI, payments to private finance contractors do not begin until the building is completed (House of Lords, 2010). This provides incentives to contractors to engage in careful planning and execution. Furthermore, the Treasury reported that there were four bidders on average for each project, signaling healthy competition. The Treasury claimed that there were no cost overruns in PFI projects, but it did not include cost overruns associated with changes in the specifications (that is, contract renegotiations). In fact, according to the figures the Treasury presented in its report, 22 percent of projects experienced increased costs because of changes in the specifications.

In a later report, the NAO shows that out of 114 projects, 69 percent were completed on time and 65 percent were within budget (NAO, 2009). However, 18 percent of projects were more than six months late, and additional projects had "late phases," presumably work ongoing after the project was delivered. The number of projects delivered at the contracted price fell to 65 percent, again as a result of changes in the design mandated by the public sector. In 20 percent of the projects, the NAO was unable to ascertain the capital costs, which could bias the conclusions. The NAO study does not present the extent of the cost overruns, so it is difficult to make comparisons with other countries. After criticism of the 2003 Treasury and NAO studies, the NAO included a special study of non-PFI projects in the 2009 report for comparison. Though the data is not totally comparable, it is much better than the comparisons in the previous reports. The differences between PFI and non-PFI performance are much smaller according to the new study because 63 percent of the 50 non-PFI projects were completed on time and 54 percent within budget, and the most likely reasons for non-compliance, once again, were design changes by the public authority.

An additional problem described in the reports was the long lead time necessary for PFI projects, which averaged 22 months (though there is no

---

[3] See Hellowell (2007) for a criticism of the methodology, however.

public sector comparator). However, long delays are likely to occur under public provision as well, had the projects been as carefully designed as under a PFI. The only delay that can be unambiguously assigned to PPPs is from arranging private financing.

Contracts are often renegotiated during the construction process, leading to increases in 35 percent of projects. In a substantial number of cases, requirements were dropped during the bidding stage and reimposed after the franchise was awarded. In this respect, PPPs have encountered this problem not only in the United Kingdom, but also in middle-income countries (see the next case study). In the case of the United Kingdom, these renegotiations and the cost escalation associated with them are partly caused by the extensive use of availability contracts, in which user fees (if they exist) only pay for operations and maintenance, and not for capital costs. When users pay fees (especially fees that are sufficient to defray the capital costs of the project), they are less willing to accept cost increases and quality reductions.

An important concern in the early part of the decade was addressing the deficiencies in the construction of the public sector comparator (PSC), which led to reforms at the time of the 2003 report. First, the discount rate was lowered from a private rate of 6 percent to 3.5 percent, which better reflected the government's borrowing cost but, as discussed in Chapter 5, biased comparisons against PFI projects. Second, there were adjustments to incorporate the taxes generated by a PFI project, which are not present under a public sector project. Third, a discount for a presumed "optimism bias" in public estimates of project costs was introduced. These two features tend to benefit PFI projects.

Another issue is contract flexibility. The government keeps the right to change any aspect of the building or service, subject to agreement with the contractor on cost. Competitive tendering is required if the change exceeds £100,000, but only occurs in 29 percent of cases. The lack of competitive bidding can be justified in some cases because the expected reduction in costs does not compensate for the additional cost of tendering, if there are known cost benchmarks and the SPV can offer expertise that no outsider has (H. M. Treasury, 2008). However, 20 percent of the changes requested by the public sector correspond to the reinstatement of requirements that were excluded from the initial contract because of their cost. The House of Commons report is correct in indicating that it is not appropriate to eliminate items at the competition stage and then reinstate them when the project has already been awarded.

Several academic studies explore the deficiencies of the PSC methodology and its supposed built-in bias toward PFI projects. Most notably, the public sector comparator remains subjective. In a detailed analysis of the VFM process in three PFI schools, Khadaroo (2008) suggests that pressure on the contracting authority led to changes in the PSC to ensure that the PFI bids would beat it, whereas small changes in assumptions would have led to public provision. This suggests that underlying the choice of PFIs is an interest in having off-balance-sheet public investments, which is confirmed by the fact that only 96 of the 667 PFI projects signed by April 2009, representing 23 percent of aggregate capital costs, were on the balance sheet. The United Kingdom's adoption of the International Financial Reporting Interpretations Committee's Interpretation 12 (IFRIC 12) in April 2009 means that all assets controlled by the public sector, which include most PPPs, will be brought on the departments' balance sheets. Yet national accounts in the United Kingdom continue to be based on the older GAAP conventions, under which most PFI projects are off budget. This has led to a situation where, following instructions from Treasury, departments are now keeping two sets of accounts, one following IFRIC 12, the other following GAAP. As long as PFI investments continue to be excluded from national debt calculations, there will be incentives to tweak VFM analysis in favor of PFI.[4]

During the past few years, there has been a strong backlash against PFI in the United Kingdom. Policy makers have discovered the hidden costs of PFI and the high rates of return for PFI investors.[5] In the new straightened conditions, the large obligations associated with PFI projects have weakened local authorities, and in cases such as the South London Healthcare Trust, they had to be put into administration. Nevertheless, the government, which is pressed for additional public investments (for needed schools to respond to the current baby boom, for example), has been trying to entice pension funds to invest in PFI projects. This would be an circuitous way of financing availability projects because it generates an obligation from the government to the pension funds that is identical to them buying government bonds and receiving quarterly coupons (but might perhaps not appear in the balance sheet as fiscal debt). In any case, in the first four months of 2012, the value of signed PFI projects had fallen by 63 percent from the already low values of the previous year.[6]

As we have noted, PFI projects reduce budgetary flexibility at the local level. Because the obligation of paying the unitary charges is contractual,

---

[4] Grimsey and Lewis (2005a) provide an extensive overview of the criticisms and problems of the PSC and the VFM approach from the point of view of practitioners.
[5] S. Neville, "Treasury urged to study PFI returns," *Financial Times*, February 10, 2012. According to the article, the NAO has found that investors selling shares early in PFI projects earn returns of 15 percent to 30 percent.
[6] G. Limmer, "PFI review leads to slump in new deals," *Financial Times*, May 11, 2012.

local public authorities cannot make reductions in the funds allocated to PFI projects. It is not clear, however, if this causes a problem or imposes useful discipline on the public sector. An evaluation of PPPs in the United Kingdom is complicated by the fact that assessments of the Private Finance Initiative appear to be biased. There is a segment of academic researchers that seems to have an ideological bias against the PFI (for example, Broadbent and Laughlin, 2005, 2008), while industry practitioners and the government, especially the Treasury, seem to have a bias in favor of PFI projects. This means that there is some tendency toward using conceptually inappropriate evaluations and searching for data that confirm preconceptions.

Summing up, in retrospect, it seems clear that the main motivation for the introduction of PPPs in the United Kingdom was to obtain a source of off-budget public investments, even though a secondary motivation may have been the potential efficiency improvements. This was done to comply with the Maastricht agreements as well as a self-imposed public debt limit of 40 percent of GDP, but it served no social purpose because the United Kingdom faced no rationing in the credit markets. As the PPPs became established, more sophisticated rationalizations were used, as embodied in the VFM concept, but the concept itself faces serious problems because of its adaptability to political requirements.

2.2 Chile

Chile now has a mature and successful highway concession system. There have been problems, however, the major one being the magnitude and generality of renegotiations of the original contracts.

History
In 1991 the Chilean congress passed a law allowing the government to award concessions for most public works, including roads, seaports, airports, reservoirs, hospitals, and jails (DFL 164 and DS 240, 1991). By the end of 2007, all main highways, most airports, and several other projects had been awarded as concessions. The total cumulative investment in 50 projects awarded by the Ministry of Public Works (known by its Spanish acronym MOP) is about $11.3 billion (U.S. billion), or less than 5 percent of current Chilean GDP (see Table 2.1). Around 88 percent of that amount has been invested in highways. This does not include seaports, which are administered under a separate concession program.

Table 2.1. *The main characteristics of the Chilean PPP system*

Type of project	Budgeted cost	Total renegotiated value	Total investment	Fraction of total	Number of works	Fraction of total	Average length of franchise
Highways (total)	185,450,742	64,286,791	249,737,533	0.88	26	0.52	27.3
Ruta 5	71,885,711	20,544,456	92,430,167	0.33	8	0.16	23.8
Interurban highways	52,951,424	10,453,407	63,404,831	0.22	13	0.26	27.7
Urban highways	60,613,607	33,288,928	93,902,535	0.33	5	0.1	31.6
Other concessions (total)	29,472,363	4,946,679	34,419,042	0.12	24	0.48	18.8
Airports	8,798,114	1,202,048	10,000,162	0.04	10	0.2	13.1
Jails	7,414,824	2,661,785	10,076,609	0.04	3	0.06	22.5
Reservoirs	4,131,579	413,094	4,544,673	0.02	2	0.04	27.5
Transantiago[a]	4,884,764	645,599	5,530,363	0.02	5	0.1	15.8
Public infrastructure	4,243,082	24,153	4,267,235	0.02	4	0.08	23.2
Total or average	214,923,105	69,233,470	284,156,575	1.00	50	1.00	22.7

Source: Engel, Fischer, Galetovic and Hermosilla and colleagues (2009).

Notes: The table reports values in unidades de fomento (UF), an inflation-indexed unit of account used in the Chilean financial system. The current exchange rate for one UF is US$43.

a. Transantiago is the public transportation system that covers Greater Santiago.

Concessions must be awarded in competitive auctions open to any firm, national or foreign. The law is flexible, leaving ample room to adapt the contract to each project. For example, the tendering variables can include user fees, a subsidy from the state, the term of the concession, income guaranteed by the state, revenue paid by the franchise holder to the state for preexisting infrastructure, risk assumed by the bidder during the construction or operation stages, quality of the technical offer, fraction of revenue (beyond a certain threshold) shared with the state (or users), and total income from the concession.

The usual procedure to finance a concession involves several stages. To begin, bidders must post contract surety bonds (*bonos de garantía*) that the government can call in if the bidder cannot finance the project. Once the concession is awarded, performance bonds are required and are callable if construction targets are not attained by predetermined dates or if quality maintenance standards are not met. Banks are the primary source of funding for the franchise holder, as the law sets conditions that make it impractical for other institutions to participate in financing road construction. Once construction is completed, the concessionaire can issue coupon bonds backed by toll revenues (securitization), which are usually bought by private pension funds and insurance companies. By law, the franchise owner cannot securitize more than 70 percent of the debt; this limit is intended to induce good behavior in the maintenance and operating phase of the franchise.

The law states that the concessionaire must build the project within the time limits established in the contract and thereafter provide uninterrupted service of a quality consistent with the terms of the bid. The MOP supervises the construction and operation of the project and has the authority to fine, suspend, or even terminate the concession should the franchise holder fail to meet its obligations. The law also establishes a dispute resolution mechanism to review conflicts between the state and the concessionaire.

Concession Program

Twenty-six highway concessions were awarded between 1993 and 2007 (see Table 2.1), involving investments of about $10 billion. Most tenders were reasonably competitive, with between three and six bidders. Projects can be classified into three groups: the Pan-American Highway (Ruta 5) between La Serena in the north and Puerto Montt in the south, which was divided into eight double-lane segments and extends over approximately 1,500 kilometers; 13 interurban highways, including some that join Santiago with nearby cities (Los Andes, San Antonio, Valparaíso) and a number of local roads (such as the La Madera road, the Nogales-Puchuncaví highway, and the northern access road into Concepción); and five urban highways in Santiago.

The program was launched in 1993 with the 23-year El Melón tunnel concession. The auction was unduly complicated (see Box 2.1), but this can be forgiven as the initial test of a new system. Subsequently, the MOP experimented with other tendering mechanisms. For example, the northern access road to Concepción, the Nogales-Puchuncaví highway, and the Santiago-San Antonio highway (Ruta 78) were awarded to the firm bidding the lowest toll.

Box 2.1 *The first Chilean concession*[7]

The auction mechanism used for the El Melón tunnel was unnecessarily complex. Firms had to bid on a weighted average of seven variables: annual subsidy by or payment to the state; toll level and structure (composed of six different tolls, with different weights for different classes of vehicles); term of the franchise; minimum income guarantee; degree of construction risk borne by the franchise holder; score on the basis of additional services; and on an inflation adjustment formula. The result of the tender was unexpected. The four firms that presented bids for the franchise demanded the maximum toll and the longest franchise term allowed by the rules of the auction. The chosen firm was decided solely based on the annual payment to the state. This outcome was inefficient because a lower toll and a smaller annual payment to the state would have been better for society. Apparently, the weights on the toll rate variable were set incorrectly. Another surprise was that the winner outbid the second highest bid by nearly a factor of three, suggesting that it was an example of the winner's curse where firms make their bids ignoring the fact that in the event that they win it is likely that their bid was optimistic about the project's profitability (Capen, Clapp, and Campbell, 1971). ∎

The tendering mechanism used for the segments of the Pan-American Highway was designed so that tolls per kilometer were similar, despite important differences in demand across segments. Firms competed on the basis of the lowest tolls for each segment, and if a lower bound (common across auctions) was reached, firms competed on either the shortest franchise term or a yearly payment to the state (which was described as a payment for preexisting infrastructure). Low-demand segments received subsidies that were financed by the annual payments from higher-demand segments.

---

[7] Based on Engel, Fischer, and Galetovic (1997a).

Table 2.2. *PVR highway concessions in Chile and winning bids*

Project	Month/year auctioned	Winning bid (million US$)[a]
Ruta 68 (Santiago–Valparaíso–Viña del Mar)	02/1998	513
Ruta 160, Coronel–Tres Pinos segment	04/2008	342
Airport access road	07/2008	56
Melipilla–Camino de la Fruta connection	08/2008	46
Ruta 5, Vallenar–Caldera segment	11/2008	288
Concepción–Cabrero highway	01/2011	318
Alternative access road, Iquique	01/2011	167

Source: MOP, Concessions Department.
Note: a. The amounts are calculated using a UF-dollar exchange rate of US$43.

The highway that joins Santiago with Valparaíso and Viña del Mar on the coast was the first that was awarded with a flexible-term PVR auction, in 1998. Under a PVR contract, the MOP sets the discount rate and the toll schedule, and the firm that bids the lowest present value of toll revenue (PVR) wins the franchise. The concession term lasts until the winning firm collects the toll revenue it demanded in its bid. Beginning in 2008, PVR auctions became the standard for awarding highway concessions in Chile: eight highway PPPs have been auctioned using this approach, with winning bids adding up to close to $2 billion (see Table 2.2 for details). In October 2010, the MOP announced a new wave of airport concessions, where concessionaires will be selected via a PVR auction. The first of four airports (Calama's El Loa) was awarded in March 2011. Chapter 3 provides a detailed analysis of PVR contracts.

The particulars of concession contracts vary, but they also share common features. Fifteen out of the 26 highway concessions have been awarded with subsidies, and 20 received minimum income guarantees. Thus, direct and contingent subsidies are almost a given when it comes to highways. At the same time, 22 highway contracts include revenue sharing between the state and the concessionaire.

One of the main virtues of the Chilean concession program is that legislation dispelled fears of expropriation. Perhaps the most evident indicator that there is little fear of expropriation is that concessionaires have been quite happy with the "build now, regulate later" approach followed by the MOP. Another merit of the Chilean Concession Law is that it specifies that all concessions must be awarded in competitive auctions open to foreign firms. This proviso limits the scope for regulatory capture and outright corruption.

An important shortcoming of the Chilean concession program, however, has been the lack of an external regulatory framework. The MOP has been in charge of designing and implementing contracts and rules defined by the specific contract. Contract enforcement is clearly undermined by the pressures for the success of a concession program measured in terms of construction, and the MOP, like most sectoral ministries under similar circumstances, has opted for development over regulation. Moreover, because the MOP renegotiates the contracts it has awarded, it can cover up mistakes, which weakens its incentives to design carefully (see Box 2.2 for an example.)

Box 2.2 *The MOP as contract supervisor*

Tribasa, a large infrastructure company, was an important participant in the first stage of Mexico's franchise program in the late 1980s, but it ran into financial problems and was bailed out by the Mexican government. Notwithstanding that experience, it became an important and aggressive participant in the initial stages of Chile's infrastructure concession program and was awarded three major franchises: the northern access road into Concepción and two segments of the Pan-American Highway (Chillán-Collipulli and Santiago-Los Vilos). As with many PPP projects in the United Kingdom, requirements were dropped during the bidding stage and reintroduced after the franchise was awarded, in so-called complementary agreements worth almost 50 percent of the original project.

After completing the northern access road into Concepción, the company ran into liquidity problems and sold the Chillán-Collipulli segment in July 1999. Moreover, the Concepción access road was plagued by unconfirmed rumors of deficient construction, and project supervisors at the MOP were investigated. In 2000, Tribasa was late in completing the stages of the Santiago-Los Vilos section of the Pan-American Highway. Surprisingly, the MOP was willing to allow the delays to accumulate without calling in the performance bonds that Tribasa had posted.[8] Eventually, public pressure forced the MOP to acknowledge a breach of contract. The MOP transferred the franchise from Tribasa to another concessionaire without a formal auction procedure. ∎

There is also evidence that the MOP has been lax in enforcing concession contracts. For example, a report issued by the Office of the Comptroller General in October 2002 concludes that the ministry relies solely on traffic data provided by franchise owners, having neglected to set up independent procedures to collect this information.[9] Government guarantees are triggered by low traffic flows, so firms have incentives to underreport traffic.

---

[8] At the time, Tribasa was filing for bankruptcy in Mexico, and later went bankrupt in Chile as well.

[9] "Contraloría critica sistema de control de concesiones," *La Tercera*, April 22, 2003.

This is particularly worrisome in the case of Route 68, in which PVR is used and the concession length is inversely related to traffic flows.

The MOP has probably auctioned projects with low social returns. The Chilean Ministry of Planning has been evaluating the social return of government-financed projects for more than three decades, thereby screening projects with low returns. As we mentioned before, the MOP seems to have subverted this procedure on occasion by removing the least cost-effective parts of the projects submitted to the Planning Ministry. The omitted components were reincorporated after the approval and adjudication of the project, via so-called complementary contracts with the franchise holder, which are negotiated bilaterally.[10]

In those cases in which subsidies have been provided, the social project evaluations that justify the subsidies have also not been made public. However, the Ministry of Finance has created a unit that analyzes the impact of the obligations incurred by the concessions program, including contingent obligations such as minimum traffic guarantees. In the report of December 2011, the estimated cost of the stock of contingent obligations associated with minimum traffic guarantees was 0.2 percent of GDP, and the estimated cost of potential conflicts with concessionaires was estimated at another 0.2 percent of GDP.

The MOP's objective of attracting bidders conflicts with the duty of the Ministry of Finance, which is responsible for the budgetary process. This has forced a more independent evaluation of the toll road program. Indeed, press reports suggest that on more than one occasion, the Ministry of Finance successfully stopped the MOP from offering particularly generous government guarantees to franchise holders. The Ministry of Finance worries that the budget will be undermined if guarantees become effective. More generally, however, the MOP can transfer rents to franchise owners via favorable regulations and lax enforcement. These transfers are unlikely to worry the Ministry of Finance as they usually do not have an impact on the budget.

Corruption in the MOP

In 2002, a case of corruption came to light in the PPP unit of the MOP. Given the number of projects awarded in the late 1990s, there was a strong demand for personnel with experience in PPPs, and the PPP unit started to lose personnel. Because of the inflexibility of Chilean government salaries, it was difficult to raise salaries legally. The PPP unit started contracting with diverse institutions, including paper firms, to provide nonexistent

[10] See "Informe de la U. de Chile revela suerte de embaucamiento del MOP a Mideplan," *La Segunda*, May 13, 2003.

services.[11] In turn, these firms and institutions would contract employees in the PPP unit without asking for any work, thus raising their effective remunerations. By this means the unit was able to retain personnel in a moment of high demand for their services in the private sector. However, these and other expenses related to the expansion of the concessions program, plus the costs associated with the commitments acquired in renegotiations, committed the budget of the MOP for several years. Because the public works was unable to obtain further funds from the finance minister, the public works minister negotiated with the PPP providers so that they would contract the paper firms to provide the nonexistent services and pay the employees of the PPP unit. The concessionaires were compensated by being allowed to overcharge in their contract renegotiations.

This was dangerous because there would be no independent checks on the private firms or the MOP. When the judges investigating a related corruption case discovered these payouts, President Lagos faced a political crisis that almost brought about his resignation, especially because he had been the previous minister of public works. Under his aegis the program had expanded considerably – which had helped him get elected – and Minister of Public Works Carlos Cruz was his instrument. The president managed to extricate himself by agreeing to a total reform of public sector hiring practices, but Minister Carlos Cruz was condemned to several years in prison.

The scandal set back the concessions program for various reasons. First, all the higher echelons of the PPP unit fell under investigation and had to resign. There were several new ministers of public works, who went into damage containment mode and had no time for reforms or new projects. Moreover, Carlos Cruz had committed all the resources of the MOP for several years, so there were no free resources to use in new studies of concession projects. As a further complication, there was a huge conflict between the MOP and the concessionaires of the prisons, where the latter used a conflict resolution mechanism biased in their favor to obtain disproportionate compensations for contractual changes ordered by the Justice Ministry, apparently without the knowledge of the MOP.

Renegotiations
During the early years of the franchise program, the government avoided renegotiations even when it would have increased welfare, as in the case of

---

[11] The fact that one of the firms involved went under the name of GATE provides one of two reasons for why the corruption case became known as MOP-GATE.

the El Melón tunnel, perhaps to build a reputation for not renegotiating. Renegotiations were thus limited until 2000, but they were then used substantially between 2001 and 2007. As of the end of 2007, the 50 concessions that the MOP awarded between 1993 and 2007 had been renegotiated 144 times. On average, a concession contract is renegotiated every two and a half years. Most renegotiations have led either to increased payments to the concessionaire for the original project or for upgrades to the original project.

Box 2.3 *Renegotiation without third-party supervision*

After signing the concession contract for Route 78, the MOP required additional works that were not included in the original contract. The franchise holder asked for compensation for the additional construction, and the ministry decided to increase tolls by 18.1 percent for a five-year period. No further explanation was given (the agreement was not publicly announced until after it was signed), and the calculations that led to the compensation were not made public.[12] ▪

Before the reforms to the law in 2010, under the Chilean concessions law, renegotiations could be either bilateral or under the supervision of a commission set up to adjudicate disputes. In a bilateral renegotiation, the MOP and the concessionaire reach an agreement that is not reviewed by an independent party. If, on the other hand, the parties fail to agree, they can appeal to a commission that first tries to conciliate and then arbitrates.[13] A little more than half of all renegotiations (74 out of 144) have been bilateral. Nevertheless, as can be deduced from Table 2.3, about 83 percent of the additional amounts conceded to concessionaires have been granted after a bilateral renegotiation, hence without external scrutiny (see Box 2.3 for an example). Almost all bilateral renegotiations have been initiated by the MOP before the project was completed. By contrast, most renegotiations with a commission have adjudicated conflicts that arose after the project was completed.

The amounts renegotiated are substantial. Of the $11.3 billion invested in 50 concessions, $2.7 billion was added after a renegotiation (see Table 2.3). At least $1.4 billion was for additional works. In other

---

[12] See "Estado compensará a privados por concesión," *El Mercurio*, July 15, 1997, page C8.

[13] Under the 2010 reforms, which are applicable only to new concessions, a permanent panel of independent experts (Panel Técnico) replaces the conciliation stage. The panel issues a recommended solution to the dispute. If one of the parties disagrees with the recommendation, the dispute proceeds to the Arbitration Commission.

Table 2.3. *Investments and renegotiations in Chilean PPPs, 1997–2007*

	(1) Number of projects and renegotiations[a]	(2) Average term (years)	(3) Original investment estimate[c]	(4) Renegotiated amounts[d]	(5) Total investment	(6) Share of total
Pan-American Highway	8/28/24[b]	23.8	2,875.43	843.46	3,718.89	0.33
Interurban	13/22/25	26.9	2,118.06	425.63	2,543.68	0.23
Urban	5/12/0	31.6	2,420.86	1,331.56	3,752.42	0.33
Highways	**26/62/49**	**26.9**	7,414.35	2,600.64	10,014.99	**0.89**
Airports	10/9/12	13.2	383.94	48.08	432.02	0.04
Jails	3/1/4	22.5	221.40	113.41	334.82	0.03
Water reservoirs	2/2/3	27.5	120.00	24.45	144.45	0.01
Public transport	5/2/2	14.7	156.81	25.82	182.64	0.02
Others	4/2/0	23.2	168.72	0.97	169.69	0.02
Other concessions	**24/16/21**	**17.5**	1,050.87	212.73	1,263.61	**0.11**
Total or average	**50/78/70**	**22.4**	8,465.22	2,813.38	11,278.59	**1**

Source: Engel, Fischer, Galetovic, and Hermosilla (2009). Reported monetary amounts in millions of U.S. dollars, converted from unidades de fomento, an inflation-indexed unit of account used in the Chilean financial system, at an exchange rate of 1 UF = 40 U.S. dollars.
Notes: a. Includes cancelled projects. b. Projects/bilateral negotiations/arbitration panels.
c. Excludes cancelled projects. d. Includes the amounts paid to cancel three concessions.

words, the total amount invested increased by about one-third after contract award.

There are several means to increase the concessionaire's revenues or compensate the firm for additional works, including direct payments from the government, tariff increases, and term extensions. The most commonly used form of compensation in Chile is a direct payment from the government, which represents almost 70 percent of the total amount renegotiated. This often does not have an immediate impact on the public budget, however. Indeed, two-thirds of these direct payments will be paid by future administrations.

Reforming the Concession Law
Several ministers after the corruption case at the MOP, Eduardo Bitrán became the new head of the MOP in March 2006. He decided to reform the legislation so as to give more control to the MOP over the projects and to reduce the extent of renegotiations of contracts. He also proposed legislation entailing a major overhaul of the governance of the public works authority, for both public provision and the PPPs. Under the proposed legislation, all infrastructure projects would specify explicit service standards that would be supervised by a new independent agency (the Infrastructure Superintendency). The proposal further specified that any renegotiations of a PPP leading to outlays in excess of 5 percent of the initial investment should be auctioned competitively and that an independent panel should be created to review all negotiations and to ensure that any contractual changes do not alter the profitability of the PPP contract (see Bitrán and Villena, 2010, for additional details).

The concession lobby strongly opposed these reforms, which resulted in the weakening of some of the provisions. Nonetheless, an important part of the reforms was approved. The administration that came into office in March 2010 had the task of implementing the provisions of the new law. The main appointees to the Ministry of Public Works provided mixed signals as to the government's interest in effective implementation of the reformed legislation. The current (mid-2012) secretary of public works is a leading presidential hopeful, and the undersecretary was previously the main legal advisor for the concession lobby. Various high-level professionals that reported to the undersecretary quit early in her tenure. The independent panels stipulated by the law have begun operating, however. And, as mentioned earlier, the government is using PVR to auction a new wave of airport concessions, a positive signal given a long history of opposition to this mechanism by the concession industry (see Chapter 3.3).

2.3 United States[14]

PPPs still are more the exception than the rule in the United States, despite a nineteenth-century tradition of privately provided public infrastructure that included private toll roads and bridges.[15] Since the early twentieth century, however, the United States has depended almost exclusively on the government for its public transport infrastructure, with the important exception of railroads. Canada, with an economy a tenth the size of that of the United States, has developed a similar number of PPP projects in recent decades. In fact, the United States has developed only 20 PPP transportation projects according to our definition.[16] See Table 2.4 for the PPP projects in the United States during the past two decades.

Several features distinguish PPPs in the United States. First, given the nation's federal organization, different states have their own approaches. The federal legislation covering PPPs is laid out in the 1998 Transportation Equity Act for the Twenty-First Century (TEA-21) and the 2005 Safe Accountable Flexible Efficient Transportation Equity Act: A Legacy for Users (SAFETEA-LU). This general enabling legislation provides guidelines for the individual states to implement PPPs, but the details, and whether to allow PPPs at all, are left to the states to decide. The federal government also allows the states to use federal funds from the 1998 Transportation Infrastructure Finance and Innovation Act (TIFIA) to leverage private investment for major transportation projects.[17]

A second characteristic of PPPs in the United States is that tax incentives play a major role. One reason PPPs have developed slowly is the tax bias in favor of traditional provision because of a well-developed debt market available to finance public investment. This bias has two main components. First, income from municipal bonds is exempt from federal taxes. Second, states face strict rules on general obligation debt but have found ways to avoid debt limits using municipal bond borrowing by public authorities. This has led to a quasi-private sector of corporate subsidiaries of state

---

[14] This section is based on Engel, Fischer, and Galetovic (2011).

[15] From the 1790s and through the first half of the nineteenth century, more than 2,000 companies sought to profit by providing road links between interior agricultural markets and ports. By 1821, they had financed, built, and operated toll roads with a combined extension of more than 10,000 miles. See Klein and Majewski (2010).

[16] As mentioned earlier in this book, our definition requires that the PPP contract include not only construction, operations, and maintenance, but also finance.

[17] Savings associated with TIFIA may be partly undone by the buy American requirement associated with federal funding. Note also that TIFIA funds tend to reduce the incentives of bidders for thorough project evaluation.

Table 2.4. *Transport PPPs in the United States, 1991–2010*

Project	State	Investment (US$ millions)	Year of financial closure	Selection process[a]	Renegotiation[b]	Current status
I-635 LBJ Managed Lanes	TX	2,800	2010	CB	No	Construction begins 2011
Denver Eagle Commuter Rail	CO	2,100	2009	CB	No	Under construction
Port of Miami Tunnel	FL	914	2009	CB	Yes	Under construction
North Tarrant Express	TX	2,047	2009	CB	No	Under construction
I-595 Managed Lanes	FL	1,814	2009	CB	No	Under construction
I-495 Beltway HOT Lanes	VA	1,998	2008	UO	PR	Under construction
SH 130 Seg. 5–6	TX	1,358	2008	CB	No	Under construction
Northwest Parkway	CO	603	2007	CB	No	Operational, went from public road to PPP
Pocahontas Parkway	VA	611	2006	UO	Yes	Near default 2005, renegotiated, expected completion 2011
Indiana Toll Road	IN	3,850	2005	CB	Yes	In operation, went from public road to PPP

Chicago Skyway	IL	1,830	2004	CB	No	Operational, went from public road to PPP
Southbay Expressway (SR 125)	CA	658	2003	CB	Yes	Operational, bankrupt 2010
Las Vegas Monorail	NV	650	2000	None	PR	Operational, bankrupt 2010
Rte. 3 Boston	MA	385	1999	CB	No	Operational
Foley Beach Express	AL	44	1999	UO	No	Operational, governor's son main proponent
Greenville Southern Connector	SC	240	1998	CB	No	Operational, bankrupt 2010
JFK Terminal 4	NY/NJ	689	1997	CB	No	Operational
Camino Colombia Toll Road	TX	85	1997	UO	No	Foreclosed 2003, repurchased by Texas DOT
Dulles Greenway	VA	350	1993	UO	Yes	See Chapter 7 for details.
Orange County SR91 Express Lanes	CA	130	1991	CB	Yes	See Chapter 7 for details.

Source: Engel, Fischer, and Galetovic (2011).
Notes: a. CB = competitive bidding. UO = unsolicited offer. PR = pending renegotiation.
b. Significant changes in initial contract terms to the advantage of the firm.

governments that build, own, operate, and finance major infrastructure
facilities off budget.

The legislative approach to PPPs varies enormously among the 31 states
that had significant PPP-enabling statutes as of April 2011 (Regulation and
Law. No. 163. C-2. August 23, 2011).[18] Legislators have a say in nine of
these states – Delaware, Florida, Indiana, Maine, Missouri, North Carolina,
Tennessee, Washington, and West Virginia – on whether some projects
are approved. The initiative with PPP projects lies mainly with state governments and the types of infrastructure that can be considered is usually
broad. Two notable exceptions are Nevada, that only considers PPP projects
proposed by the private sector, and Kansas, that only has enabling legislation for innovative pavement management projects.

Most of the early projects were either unsolicited bids (for example, the
Dulles Greenway in Virginia in 1993, the Pocahontas Parkway in Virginia,
originally proposed in 1998, and the Camino Colombia in Texas of 1997) or
collaborations with a private party (for example, the Orange County State
Route 91 high-occupancy toll lanes in 1995, the Greenville Southern
Connector in South Carolina, and the Northwest Parkway in Colorado).
All in all, 6 out of the 20 existing PPP projects in the United States were
awarded without competition. More recent cases have all been awarded
competitively. There has been learning from experience.

Several of the early projects were unsuccessful and had to renegotiate
their contracts or went into default. In one case, the PPP was foreclosed.
When projects run into trouble, contracts are usually renegotiated. One
distinguishing characteristic of the United States is that there is no specific
conflict resolution framework for PPPs, except that provided by legislation
regarding infrastructure in general.

Efficiency

We have emphasized the importance of bundling construction and maintenance as an important source of efficiency gains in PPPs (see Chapter 1.4).
We are not aware of studies illustrating the quantitative importance of bundling. Nevertheless, the United States provides anecdotal evidence that PPPs
can lower construction and operating costs. For example, the concessionaire that built express lanes on State Route 91 in Orange County, California,
reduced construction time substantially by innovating in traffic management during construction (see Small, 2010, working paper version). Also,

---

[18] Iseki and colleagues (2009), Rall, Reed, and Farber (2010), and Nossaman (2011) describe
U.S. PPP legislation.

the consortium that proposed the I-495 Capital Beltway high-occupancy toll lanes (HOT) in Fairfax County, Virginia, built the lanes for one-third of the cost of the high-occupancy vehicle (HOV) lanes then planned by the Virginia Department of Transportation (Poole, 2006).

In the case of the Chicago Skyway, operating costs were reduced by 11 percent, in real terms, relative to the previous four years under city management (average traffic was similar in both four-year periods). Most of the improvement was due to the replacement of city workers with non-unionized workers who were paid market rates. Because the concession agreement allowed existing employees to move to other public jobs and 95 percent of the workers chose this option, overall efficiency probably fell (see Box 2.4 for details). In general, PPPs often lead to efficiency gains because they allow firms to circumvent the provisions of the Davis-Bacon Act that imposes a floor on wages for public sector construction workers. In fact, the most recent attempt at passing a bill authorizing PPPs in Pennsylvania in early 2011 failed because the business community objected to provisions requiring the payment of "prevailing wages" (Regulation and Law. No. 163. C-8. August 23, 2011).

Tolls

Most highway PPPs in the United States derive their revenue from tolls, with the significant exception of a few projects that receive availability payments in Colorado, Florida, and Massachusetts.[19] This raises a frequent criticism of PPPs in terms of their impact on different income segments. For example, the HOT lanes built under PPPs are occasionally labeled "Lexus lanes." More generally, the argument is that toll roads are unfair to lower-income users. This is an argument for rationing (by congestion) and against a market solution, which is incorrect in the case of greenfield or brownfield projects (see the introduction). More to the point, there is little evidence of a preponderance of expensive cars among users. A study of the State Route 167 HOT lanes in Washington State showed that the most common makes of car using the lanes were Ford, Chevrolet/GMC, Toyota, Honda, and Dodge.

Apart from their distributional impact, tolls and user fees can also lead to more efficient outcomes by reducing excessive congestion on a facility. One of the weaknesses of government control of toll highways is the tendency to

---

[19] The exceptions are the Port of Miami Tunnel, the I-595 corridor in Florida, the Eagle Commuter Rail Project in Denver, Colorado, and the Route 3 in Boston, Massachusetts.

keep tolls at an inefficiently low level, as illustrated by the Chicago Skyway (see Box 2.4) and the Indiana toll road (see Section 1.4).

White Elephants

As described earlier, one of the arguments for PPPs is that under certain conditions they filter white elephants. This will not be the case, however, if the projects are financed with subsidies or if there is an implicit guarantee that the government will bail out a troubled concessionaire. A thorough cost-benefit analysis should therefore be undertaken for all infrastructure projects.[20] In the United States, many federal infrastructure projects are not subject to cost-benefit analysis, which explains the pork-barrel projects that are so dear to the federal legislature.

Several PPP projects defaulted in the United States. The first PPP project, the Dulles Greenway in Virginia, opened in 1993 and sought refinancing in 1999 (see Chapter 7). The South Bay Expressway in San Diego, California, opened in 2007 and filed for Chapter 11 in March 2010, citing traffic at less than 40 percent of initial projections. This PPP came out of Chapter 11 proceedings in May 2011, under the ownership of senior creditors. One of these is the federal government, which took a 42 percent haircut on the $172 million (U.S. million) loan it made under TIFIA. Similarly, the Camino Colombia toll road in Texas was foreclosed by a district court in 2003 – the only such case in the United States – as effective revenues were only 6 percent of those estimated. In 2010, the Greenville Southern Connector in South Carolina filed for Chapter 9. A demand forecast study predicted revenues of $14 million by 2007, whereas actual revenue was only $5.4 million. The road made no sense as an access road to local commercial developments: traffic barely justified a two-lane road, let alone the four-lane expressway that was actually built, suggesting that this project qualifies as a white elephant.

The Greenville Southern Connector is one of three so-called 63–20 projects (thus named for the type of tax-exempt municipal financing they had access to originally) that went bankrupt.[21] These projects were enthusiastically promoted by a combination of consultants, engineering firms,

---

[20] It can be argued that a project that is fully financed by user fees and for which there is no expectation of renegotiation does not require cost-benefit analysis because it will be privately profitable in all scenarios without public resources. Nonetheless, a cost-benefit analysis may be justified in this case as well because negative externalities could make a project privately but not socially attractive.

[21] The 63–20 tax exemption allows for nonprofit infrastructure projects by public-private associations.

financiers, and construction firms, who made money at the expense of
bondholders during the development, design, and construction phases and
had nothing at stake thereafter.[22] As with the London Underground PPP, a
poor incentive structure was central to the projects' failure.

Renegotiations

Table 2.4 shows that 40 percent of PPPs in the U.S. transport sector have
undergone major renegotiations. The first case was the aforementioned
Dulles Greenway project in Virginia that defaulted on its bond holdings
in 1999 because of overoptimistic demand forecasts. It was followed by the
express lane of California's State Route 91, where demand grew much faster
than expected but a non-compete clause prevented the government from
franchising (or building) additional lanes. The absence of an early termination option caused protracted negotiations that lasted for several years
and eventually led to the buyout of the concessionaire by a state agency. As
discussed in detail in Section 7.3, these renegotiations illustrate many of the
problems posed by renegotiations of PPP contracts as well as how flexible-
term contracts can mitigate these problems.

Anticipating Spending

The Chicago Skyway and the Indiana Toll Road are examples of a PPP-type
contract used to lease an existing facility.[23] In both cases, the contract was
used to anticipate government spending. This practice usually reduces welfare, but unexpectedly high bids suggest that the City of Chicago and the
State of Indiana are likely to be better off. The short-term political benefits
of these projects were important.

In Chicago, a portion of the lease payment was set aside to retire outstanding Skyway bonds and city debt or to go into the long-term reserve.
The remainder had almost all been spent before Mayor Richard Daley
retired in 2010. See Box 2.4 for details.

In Indiana, the results were similar. The Indiana Toll Road, which is part
of the U.S. Interstate Highway System, runs for 157 miles (253 km) and
connects the Chicago Skyway to the Ohio Turnpike. A consortium of the
same firms that leased the Chicago Skyway paid $3.8 billion for a 75-year
lease of the Indiana Toll Road. This sum was much larger than the estimates
of a state-commissioned analysis, which valued future cash flows at $1.9

---

[22] See www.tollroadsnews.com/node/4808.
[23] The Indiana Toll Road contract includes a commitment by the leaseholder to invest
      $770 million (U.S. million) in improvements, so it is partially a brownfield project.

billion. Part of the difference is due to the economies of having both highways under a single administration, even though it is not obvious why the
concessionaire would include what appears to be a large fraction of these
rents in its bid. Clearly there was also an element of winner's curse, and the
owners have since written down the capital value of the concession.

   ·   In both these cases, politicians managed to convert future revenues
into current spending, and they were fortunate that the winning bid was
much higher than the value of the road (see Box 2.4). This allowed them
to develop a reputation for prudence by using part of the resources to pay
down debt and invest for the long term, while using the windfall to increase
current expenditures. Perhaps the most significant feature of leases, at least
in the case of the Chicago Skyway, was that the City of Chicago managed to
enhance the value of its asset by committing to higher tolls.

Box 2.4 *The Chicago Skyway*[24]

The Chicago Skyway is a 7.8-mile (12.6 km), six-lane, median-divided toll road in
Chicago, Illinois, which links downtown Chicago to the Illinois-Indiana state line.
The City of Chicago initially developed the Skyway in 1959, with bond financing
linked to toll revenue. However, the city was unable to raise tolls enough to service
the debt and the courts ordered it to increase user fees. Even then, the first principal
payment (after paying off all interest due) was only made in 1991, when the financial situation of the project improved because of congestion on alternative non-toll
roads. After retiring the original bonds in 1994, the city made no further toll adjustments until it leased the project in 2005.

   After 1994 the city started using the revenue from the Skyway to fund other
transportation projects and began to anticipate the revenues from the Skyway by
issuing bonds in 1996 for the same purpose. In 2004, the city issued a Request for
Qualifications that brought in five qualified bidders for a 99-year lease of the Chicago
Skyway. The bidders competed for the operations and maintenance of the highway
in exchange for toll revenues according to a predetermined toll schedule. There were
three active bidders, with an undisclosed reservation price estimated to lie between
$700 million and $800 million. The winning bid of $1.83 billion was submitted by
Cintra-Maquarie. The other two bids were well under a billion dollars, providing
some indications of the winner's curse. Cheng (2010) estimates that under all reasonable demand scenarios, Cintra-Maquarie paid too much for the project.

   Three points stand out from this case study. First, major toll increases were pushed
into the future, past the end of the then-current mayor's term of office. Second, before
leasing the Skyway, the city procured an exemption from leasehold taxes for the facility, thus raising its current value at the expense of future revenues. Finally, the lease
term proposed originally was 55 years, but the actual lease considered in the contract

---

[24] Based Cheng (2010).

was 99 years at the insistence of potential bidders. A possible explanation for the insistence of bidders for an extremely long lease term could be associated tax advantages. A private entity with a sufficiently long lease gains asset ownership and can include depreciation as an expense for federal tax purposes. As reported in the company's financial statement, the depreciation expense for 2009 and 2010 amounted to $18.9 million for the Chicago Skyway.[25] Cheng (2010) shows that the PPP was financially convenient for the city, because only under implausibly optimistic expectations of traffic growth and an undemonstrated ability to raise tolls would it have been able to generate the amount of discounted revenue it received from the winning bid. There are other potential efficiency gains from private management (more efficient maintenance and operations), but their impact is relatively minor (operating costs fell by 11 percent, a gain of $1 million a year). Efficiency gains should thus have a correspondingly small impact on the overall valuation of the facility.

The short-term political benefits of the program were important. Part of the debt was used to retire Skyway bonds and city debt, and $500 million was put into a long-term reserve. The remaining $475 million went into discretionary funds, of which the city had spent 83 percent by 2010. ∎

Future Prospects

According to the nonpartisan Congressional Budget Office (CBO, 2008), current spending and investment in highways in the United States is less than one-third of the amount needed to maintain current levels of service and to finance investments whose private and social benefits exceed their economic costs ($66.7 billion versus $210.5 billion for 2004). The highway deficit is reflected, for example, in an increase in the cost of congestion in metropolitan areas from $20 billion in the early 1980s to $120 billion in recent years (Lomax, Schrank, and Turner, 2010).

The lack of resources for infrastructure improvement extends across all sectors, from levees to wastewater treatment, and from transportation to schools. According to the Federal Highway Administration (FHWA), as of December 2010 more than 145,000 bridges in the United States were classified as either structurally deficient or structurally obsolete (FHWA, 2011).[26] The American Society of Civil Engineers estimates that, as a result of

---

[25] For the Indiana Toll Road, depreciation expenses during 2009–2010 added to $73.6 million.

[26] A structurally deficient bridge requires significant maintenance and repair to remain in service while a structurally obsolete bridge has a design not suitable for its current use. Note, however, that the share of deficient bridges fell from 34.6 percent in 1992 to 26.5 percent in 2009. The absolute numbers of deficient bridges have increased in the period, however, from 156,863 to 159,859. In effect, new bridges are built but deficient ones are not repaired (FHWA Conditions and Performance Reports, 1999, 2010).

decades of insufficient investment, the infrastructure deficit in the United States amounts to $2.2 trillion.

However, government spending in coming years is unlikely to reduce the infrastructure deficit, as federal and state governments struggle with large debt burdens. The federal government can, in principle, run deficits to spend on sorely needed infrastructure, yet the prevailing political climate casts doubt on the use of this option. State and local governments, which finance approximately half of spending on highways, face an even more daunting challenge, as balanced budget requirements leave less space for debt financing of infrastructure in their case. With projected outlays for entitlements, such as health care and retirement benefits, looming large in the near future, and revenue from sales, income, and especially property taxes expected to remain depressed for some time, state and local governments face an even larger challenge than the federal government when funding infrastructure.

Given the perceived lack of public resources, public-private partnerships may emerge as an attractive option to finance needed infrastructure and avoid a major drag on economic growth in coming years. It is therefore not surprising that the number of states with enabling statutes for PPPs jumped from 23 to 31 between 2005 and 2011 (Regulation and Law. No. 163. C-2. August 23, 2011). Even though ultimately resources to finance new projects always come from user fees and taxes, the fact that governments do not need to make upfront payments under PPPs makes this option attractive in the current political climate. As mentioned in Section 1.4 and further discussed in Chapter 6, strained government budgets seldom offer an economic rationale in favor of PPPs, the current U.S. situation being no exception. However, if institutions and contracts are designed incorporating the lessons from recent decades, the efficiency gains PPPs can attain could be substantial and end up legitimizing this organizational form. Even though the United States may end up choosing PPPs for the wrong reason, it could turn out to be the right choice.

2.4 China

The rapid growth of China has led to huge demands for infrastructure services throughout the country. Some of these, such as the 65,000-kilometer National Expressway Network, were built with centralized funding as part of a national plan. Another significant fraction of infrastructure – especially in services – was provided by state companies, though the use of state companies for this purpose has been declining in recent years. At the national level, a large fraction of GDP is assigned to infrastructure investment, reaching 12 percent during 2008. Infrastructure spending (in real terms) in the 2004–2008 period was higher than in the entire twentieth century.[27] Road investment has grown at a particularly high rate.

Despite the importance of central government spending on infrastructure, most of the responsibility for building infrastructure projects lies with the regional and local governments. The demand for infrastructure is due, in part, to the demands of urbanization. China is still a rural country, with an urbanization level of only 40 percent in 2003 (Ho, 2006), yet 20 million villagers move into the cities each year, creating the need for new infrastructure and services.

This rapid growth requires increased provision of energy and additional and better roads, railways, seaports, and airports, as well as other infrastructure facilities. However, the local and regional governments face serious financial constraints. Prior to the decentralization process that began in 1980 and is still ongoing, the fiscal system featured a centralized collection of fiscal revenues, which were then allocated and transferred to regions (Wu, 2010). This meant that the resources necessary for building and maintaining infrastructure were not easily available to the regions and local governments.[28]

The situation has improved somewhat. Since 1994, the local governments have been assigned some local tax collection and spending power. However, these resources have not been sufficient for the large needs of urban infrastructure investment, and this has forced local and regional governments to find other sources of finance. A small share of funding is generated through user and connection fees. More important, land transfer fees provide 11 percent of the revenues assigned to urban construction and maintenance, and more than 30 percent comes from internal loans. Finally, local governments have used PPPs to finance infrastructure.

Table 2.5 shows the case of transport infrastructure, in terms of both the total amounts invested and their proportion of total public investment. It also presents a decomposition of investment by the various types of projects. Highway investment is, by far, the most important component of public infrastructure. Finally, the table decomposes the sources of funds for transport infrastructure. The main source of funds is internal savings. Table 2.6 goes into more detail by decomposing road investment into various categories. As the table illustrates, the major increase in infrastructure

---

[27] "Building BRICS of Growth," Economic focus. *The Economist*, June 5, 2008.
[28] See, for example, KPMG (2009) and Wu (2010).

Table 2.5. *Investment in transport infrastructure in China*

Investment	Year						
	2000	2001	2002	2003	2004	2005	2006
Total investment in transport fixed assets ($ billion)	41.50	47.70	55.00	61,30	76.10	90.20	103.41
Investment in transport fixed assets (percentage of total public investment)	NA	NA	9.83%	8.75%	8.62%	7.27%	6.72%
Grouped by function:							
Ports and other coastal construction	2.4%	3.2%	3.1%	4.9%	5.5%	8.0%	9.9%
Inland waterway construction	1.6%	1.3%	0.9%	1.1%	1.2%	1.6%	2.3%
Highway construction	68.9%	69.1%	72.1%	74.8%	76.3%	76.0%	87.3%
Railways	23.5%	23.2%	21.6%	16.7%	13.7%	10.7%	N/A
Others	3.6%	3.2%	2.3%	2.6%	3.4%	3.8%	4.0%
Grouped by source of funds (excluding railways):							
State budget	12.4%	15.4%	19.3%	15.5%	14.3%	15.2%	15.2%
Domestic loans	34.2%	38.4%	41.0%	41.3%	40.4%	45.1%	45.1%
Foreign investment	3.7%	3.1%	2.7%	2.6%	1.3%	2.0%	2.0%
Self financing and others	49.8%	43.1%	37.0%	40.6%	44.0%	37.6%	39.6%

Source: Rui (2008), from the *Chinese Transport Statistical Yearbook*, 2006.

occurred in rural roads, which are important for reducing poverty and promoting growth in those areas.

PPPs in China

The first Chinese PPP project was the Shajiao B power plant in Shenzhen, in operation since 1988 (although power plant PPPs are not included in our definition of PPP). Because of lack of experience, the project was unsuccessful in the sense that the allocation of risk was too favorable for the private party (Ke et al., 2010). Since then, there have been two rounds of PPPs. The first, which was directed mostly at the water and power sectors, ended with the decade of the 1990s (see Figure 2.2). The central

Table 2.6. *Road infrastructure investment in China (USD millions)*

Year	Roads, rural	Key roads	Road upgrades	Total roads
2001	4,353	13,906	14,027	32,285
2002	6,046	15,599	17,170	38,815
2003	9,915	16,445	18,622	44,982
2004	14,994	21,161	20,677	56,832
2005	16,929	19,226	18,138	54,293
2006	20,075	39,147	19,072	78,294
2007	24,179	42,707	18,397	85,283
2008	29,545	43,958	25,654	99,157

Source: *China Statistical Yearbook*, 2001–2008, as cited in KPMG (2009).

government then decided to invest large amounts in infrastructure and at the same time "to clean up the unregulated and illegal projects" (see Ke, Wang, and Chan, 2009, p. 3), even to the extent of demolishing illegal projects (Cheng and Wang, 2009). However, the central resources were insufficient to finance these projects, and a new wave of PPPs started in the early 2000s, including almost half of the Olympic arenas in Beijing. Most of the investments in the second wave of PPPs were concentrated in toll roads, water and sewerage projects, and city gas. In terms of transport infrastructure (that is, bridges, roads, tunnels, seaports, and airports), total investment in the period 2000–2010 amounted to almost $24 billion. The characteristics of these PPP projects are described in Table 2.7.

The amount invested in these projects varies considerably, as illustrated in Figure 2.3. The data do not show a trend, but then we are only looking at transport projects. An interesting development is the increase in PPPs that are assigned by competitive bidding, as opposed to direct negotiation or competitive negotiation. Only 3 out of 22 PPPs were assigned by competitive auction in 2000–2004, versus 16 out of 56 PPPs in the succeeding five years. The share of PPPs assigned competitively thus more than doubled, from 13.6 percent to 28.6 percent.

Problems of PPPs in China

While the central Chinese government is willing to accept PPP investment, and local and regional governments need PPP investment to achieve their infrastructure targets, the Chinese legal and political environment has dangerous pitfalls. The Chinese PPP experience includes examples of PPP firms

Table 2.7. *Characteristics of Chinese PPPs in the transport sector, 2000–2010*

Project type	Number	Percentage	Term length (years)		Cost (MMUS$)	
			Average	Median	Average	Median
Bridges	4	5	27.5	27.5	429.2	93.1
Seaports	35	45	48.0	50.0	282.2	175.0
Highways	28	36	26.5	27.0	347.0	227.1
Airports	4	5	31.3	25.0	41.1	41.1
Railroads	6	8	30.0	30.0	553.0	654.9
Canal	1	1	30.0	30.0	47.0	30.0
All projects	78	100	36.8	30.0	326.6	206.4

Source: Authors, using data from World Bank PFI.

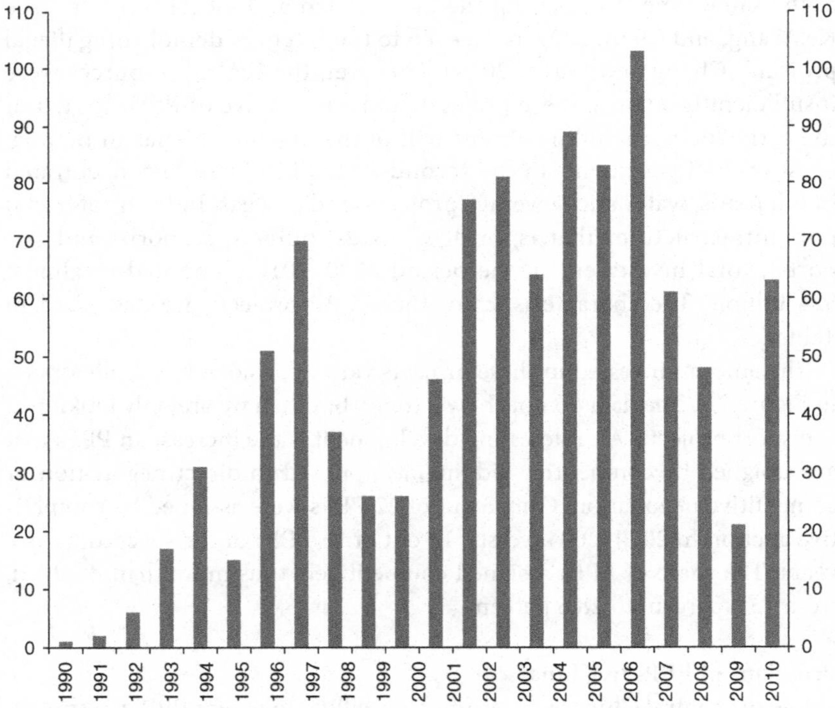

Figure 2.2. Number of PPI projects, 1990–2011.
Source: World Bank and PPIAF, PPI database.
Note: Includes management contracts, BOO, merchant and divestiture, that is, uses a broader definition of PPP than that used in this book. In this case, the quantitative differences with our definition are minor.

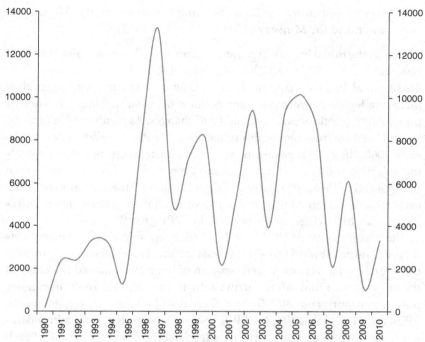

Figure 2.3. Total investment commitments, 1990–2011 (in millions of US$).
Source: World Bank and PPIAF, PPI database.
Note: Includes management contracts, BOO, merchant and divestiture, that is, uses a broader definition of PPP than that used in this book. In this case, the differences with our definition are minor.

exploiting users and of local governments expropriating firms that have "too high a rate of return" (Ke et al., 2009, p. 185).

In the first wave of PPP projects that ended in 1998–1999, the legal environment for PPPs was weakly defined. The legal environment mainly consisted in the following documents (Cheng and Wang, 2009; Ke et al., 2009):

1. Local administrative measures on the concession of municipal public utilities in Huer-haote and Hainan (1994);
2. Circular of the Ministry of Foreign Trade and Economic Cooperation Concerning the Absorption of Foreign Investment by means of BOT (1995);
3. Circular on Several Issues Concerning the Examination, Approval, and Administration of Experimental Foreign-Invested Concession

Projects, issued by the State Planning Commission, the Ministry of Power, and the Ministry of Transportation (1995).[29]

Hence, the initial legal document was a provincial measure allowing concessions. To date, China still has no national legislation concerning PPPs. These initial PPPs – many of them in utilities – ran into severe trouble, including legislative changes, poor political decision making, government unreliability, public opposition, and tariff changes. As mentioned before, the institutional environment in this initial stage of PPPs was thus very risky. In early 2000, the central government chose infrastructure as a major spending objective and decided to curtail and even to close down or expropriate unregulated or illegal PPP projects (Ke et al., 2009). However, as mentioned earlier, the government was unable to satisfy all the requirements of infrastructure, which triggered a new period of PPP growth.

The second wave of PPPs involved relatively fewer utility projects, as their use shifted toward transport infrastructure. Nevertheless, only in 2005 did the central government first issue an opinion that allowed the entry of the private sector into infrastructure activities such as telecommunications, power, transport, and oil.[30] To date, there is still no national law governing PPPs, and the legal setting for PPPs rests on various legal and administrative decisions at the local and regional levels, some of which contradict each other. For example, Cheng and Wang (2009) claim that the two 1995 statutes cited earlier are in conflict regarding risk allocation and government guarantees, while the local governments' use of guarantees for PPPs goes against the central government prohibition on using government guarantees to attract investment.

Another risk affecting PPPs is the fact that bureaucratic decisions trump local judicial and legislative decisions. Moreover, the so-called collusion between the local or regional public sector and businesses at the expense of the public can lead to protests and central government interventions. These relationships between business and local government officials include personal ties and reciprocal exchanges of favors and benefits, which weaken legal rules (Cheng and Wang, 2009). According to the Chinese National Audit Office (2008), 64 out of 106 leased projects that were audited showed signs of corruption (Rui, de Jong, and ten

---

[29] Additional circulars and temporary measures dealt with the issue of foreign exchange in BOT projects.

[30] Several Opinions of the State Council on Encouraging, Supporting and Guiding the Development of Individual and Private Economy and Other Non-Public Sectors of the Economy; see Ke and colleagues (2009).

Heuvelhof, 2008).[31] Given these risks and the fact that local politicians have short-term interests that depend on central government policy decisions, investors feel the need for support letters from the upper levels of government, again a weak guarantee.

Rui, de Jong, and ten Heuvelhof (2010) describe cases of corruption (such as the He-Chao-Wu Expressway in Anhui province), of unfair competition with the PPP (for example, the Citong Bridge in Fujian province), and other problems (such as an excessive number of free passes issued for the Xiang-Jing Expressway). We describe these cases later in this chapter (Boxes 2.5, 2.6, and 2.7), following the description in Rui (2008), while Box 2.8 illustrates the learning process under way in the case of subway PPPs. Regarding maintenance and operations, the authors report that the Chinese Audit Office has discovered many cases of strategically reduced maintenance of roads in places where it is difficult to supervise. Finally, unauthorized tollbooths are common on PPP roads: the Chinese National Audit Office has found 158 illegal tollbooths in 16 (out of 18) provinces that were investigated.

Box 2.5 *A case of corruption: the He-Chao-Wu Expressway in Anhui province*

The He-Chao-Wu Expressway is a lease project (which the Chinese call a transfer-operate-transfer, or TOT). It was a brownfield transfer of the facility to a private firm for a number of years in exchange for a large lump sum. The He-Chao-Wu Expressway PPP model is similar to the Chicago Skyway in that the local government transferred an existing facility to a private firm to operate and maintain for a period of time in exchange for toll revenue, after which it would be transferred back to the government. The private firm put up a large amount for the contract, a sum that the local government wanted to use for other, supposedly more productive, purposes. In this case, the state company, Anhui Expressway Company, transferred the expressway (without open bidding) to the private firm Shanghai Eastern Holdings Limited (SEHL) in exchange for $230 million (plus an expected $72 million in maintenance expenses over the duration of the contract) to be paid in 2003.

Two years later, the local government bought back the expressway at a price of $433 million. SEHL had gone into bankruptcy, and because the asset could not be transferred to a third party, the only way to continue operations was to buy back the project. However, the price paid was almost double the original amount. In its 2008 investigation, the Chinese National Audit Office found evidence of corruption: public officials, paid by SEHL, had lowered the valuation of the project so that SEHL could get the franchise at a low price. ∎

---

[31] In his doctoral thesis, Rui (2008) mentions "different types of problems" rather than citing corruption specifically, as in Rui and colleagues (2008).

Box 2.6 *A case of unfair competition in Fujian province*

The 1,503-meter-long Citong Bridge was the first PPP/BOT bridge in China. It was designed by the Quanzhou local government of Fujian province to complement the existing Quanzhou Bridge, which was congested. Fifteen small local firms grouped together and proposed to build the Citong Bridge, and the project was awarded without tendering. The local government subsidized 40 percent of the $30 million project, which has a 30-year concession term. Just one year after opening in 1996, the Citong Bridge toll revenue had already reached $12 million, making it a very profitable project.

However, the decentralization process then in progress transferred the Quanzhou Bridge toll revenue to the local government, which was now competing for revenues with the Citong Bridge. To sabotage its rival, the Quanzhou government built a connecting link from the Quanzhou Bridge to two new important highways, and it refused to allow the Citong Bridge owners to build a similar connection, even though the concessionaires would build it at their own expense. Eventually, after applying to the Fujian province government, the Citong Bridge operators were able to build a link to one (and only one) of the two new highways, but it had to be built S-shaped because the Quanzhou link interfered with the original design for a straight connection. The other important road is still not connected. ∎

Box 2.7 *A case of hidden expropriation: the Xiang-Jin Expressway in Hubei province*

The Xiang-Jin Expressway was the first BOT expressway project in China. It is 185 kilometers long and was budgeted to cost $542 million. Construction began in early 2001, and the expressway opened to traffic in June 2004. The Hubei Xiang-Jing Expressway company won the competitive bidding process and will operate the road for the 35-year concession period. The contract established lower (guaranteed with subsidies) and maximum (when profit-sharing begins) profit rates for the firm. According to the Chinese National Audit Office, there were no construction problems, even though the project was built ahead of time and under cost (by 17.8 percent). Despite these encouraging successes, the concessionaire faced problems with toll collection. Specifically, the Hubei provincial government has issued an excessive number of free toll cards. By 2007, almost 10,000 cars were not paying tolls on the highway, and the estimated losses for the period 2006–2008 exceeded $5 million – approximately 1 percent of the private firm's investment. When the company complained, the government evaded responsibility, and the firm continues to face a drain of revenues from the excessive number of free passes. ∎

Box 2.8 *A case of learning: lines 4 and 5 of the Beijing metro*[32]

As part of the broad development of its metro system, in 2001 the Beijing government proposed Line 5, a 28-kilometer route traversing central Beijing. A BOT contract with an operating period of 25 years was awarded to a joint venture between SNC-Lavalin of Canada and three domestic companies, following international competitive bidding. Before financial closure, SNC-Lavalin negotiated that the Beijing government would pay for hard infrastructure (such as earthworks and tunnels), while the joint venture would invest in railways and vehicles. The Beijing government orally agreed to SNC-Lavalin's terms, and construction was started with public funds. However, before the contract was finalized in late 2001, the firms composing the concessionaire had serious disagreements and failed to form an SPV. Bank loans saved the project, and a domestic company obtained the service contract to operate the project in closed negotiations. Line 5 opened in 2007.

The experience with Line 5 influenced the planning of Line 4. The 30-year BOT contract for the 28-kilometer route was competitively awarded in 2006 to a joint venture, but only after an initial prescreening of candidates. The winning joint venture proposed a clear financial structure, with provisions to transfer excess profits back to the Beijing government. The contract also stipulated the government provision of hard infrastructure, as previously negotiated for Line 5. Line 4 was completed in 2009, on time and on budget. These metro cases reflect government learning regarding roles and duties in PPPs, which contributes to more predictable and favorable PPP outcomes. ▪

Box 2.9 *A case of excess: the Qingdao Bay Bridge*

The Qingdao Bay Bridge is the longest bridge ever built. It is a six-lane bridge, with a length of 41 kilometers, which crosses Jiaozhou Bay, between the Qingdao and Hungdao districts in China. It was built in four years at an estimated cost of $2.3 billion (though there are other, much higher, cost estimates). It is interesting to note that it serves basically the same market as the six-lane Qingdao Jiaozhou Bay Tunnel, which opened the same day. Not too far away, and running parallel to the bridge, a highway links the two districts. Adding 12 lanes of highway in one day meant that traffic was far below expectations at 10,000 versus the estimated 30,000 daily. The idea of building the bridge, according to the *Financial Times*, came from a local Communist Party chief who lost his job shortly thereafter because of corruption.[33] ▪

---

[32] Based on de Jong and colleagues (2010).

[33] S. Rabinovich, "China: The road to nowhere," *Financial Times*, July 16, 2012. The article also mentions the possibility of shoddy construction.

Summing up, PPPs are an important factor in infrastructure in China, and they appear attractive to investors. There are two reasons for this interest. First, households face negative real rates in the financial sector, so resources are available for alternative investments like PPPs even when they offer negative, though higher, expected returns. In China, households account for 30 percent of revenues used for investment in so-called urban maintenance and construction, that is, public utilities and municipal works, including roads and sanitation (Wu, 2010; also see Table 2.5). Second, for international investors, the rapid growth rates in China are attractive despite the risks involved in infrastructure investments.

Nevertheless, there are severe deficiencies in the Chinese environment for PPPs. The lack of a strong rule of law (as evidenced by the fact that that there is no law covering PPPs) increases the risk for investors and the public. Monitoring mechanisms are insufficient, and local authorities tend to abuse their power, either by aiding businessmen (illegal tollbooths should be easily detected) or by expropriating them through various means, with little possibility of effective recourse to judicial authority. Furthermore, concerns are growing about the quality of materials used during construction and the extent to which projects are properly engineered, triggered by the collapse of six large bridges in less than a year.[34] There have been some noteworthy advances. First, authorities at the central level have written favorable statements ("opinions") on private investment in infrastructure, though these opinions are not binding for the central level itself. Second, competitive bidding has become more common, at least in the case of transport infrastructure. Finally, the regional and local governments have learned from experience, resulting in fewer cases of failed PPPs.

2.5 Conclusion

As mentioned in the introduction to this chapter, these four country studies highlight different aspects of the PPP experience that will be analyzed in detail in the chapters that follow.

In the United Kingdom, the main motivation for PPPs seems to have been the desire to elude the public investment restrictions incorporated in the Maastricht Treaty. This is the reason the Ryrie Rules, which limited spending on PPPs by reducing public spending by the same amount, were

---

[34] See Keith Bradscher, "Collapse of new bridge underscores worries about China infrastructure," *New York Times*, August 24, 2012 and Fernando Fuentes, "Colapso de puente inaugurado hace nueve meses desata críticas en China," *La Tercera*, August 25, 2012, p. 43.

dropped in 1989 (see Box 6.2). In its place, the United Kingdom introduced the concept of Value for Money, a subjective methodology, to help decide if an infrastructure project was to be provided through PPPs or by public provision, that is, as public spending. In Chapter 6 we analyze the public finance of PPPs, which is directly related to the points raised by this case.

The United States shows that even in developed countries, infrastructure quality can deteriorate due to a lack of sufficient new investment in infrastructure, leading to congestion and obsolescence of infrastructure. Moreover, state and local governments have been laggard in raising tolls, which means that the real value of toll revenues from existing state and locally owned infrastructure projects has fallen. As the budgetary restrictions at the state and local levels become binding, PPPs may help to provide additional infrastructure, because their contracts include commitments to tolls indexed to inflation and also solve the maintenance problem. However, in many cases the temptation of state governments to use PPPs to anticipate spending is also apparent and needs to be addressed.

The case of Chile highlights two important issues: the negative role of renegotiations and, linked to this issue, the possibilities of corruption when the PPP system expands rapidly. While some contract renegotiations are justified, others serve to cover up mistakes by the public works authority or are used to spend more in infrastructure than authorized by Congress. This case also shows how legal reforms can improve on the deficiencies of the PPP institutional setting. Some of these problems are covered in Chapter 4 while others are analyzed in Chapter 8.

Finally, the case of China shows that a well-defined and specific legal environment is needed for a PPP system that works well. In China, the excess accumulation of savings and the high growth rates meant that even though this framework was lacking, investors were willing to take the risks of participating in PPPs even in projects that have all the appearance of being white elephants. More recently, advances have taken place in institutions and procedures that bode well for the future of PPPs in China, but the industry faces a difficulty due to the current overinvestment in infrastructure. In any case, in most countries, well-designed rules are needed for the development of PPPs and to obtain their advantages over other forms of infrastructure provision.

3

Highways

The type of infrastructure for which PPPs have been used most – in Europe, developing countries, and the United States – is highways. In this chapter we answer the questions of when and how PPPs are appropriate for this particular kind of infrastructure.

Ideally, the best organizational form – whether traditional, PPP, or privatization – for providing a specific infrastructure should be determined by the project's physical and economic characteristics. If political economy considerations are important – for example, opposition to privatization or to paying user fees – then the choice should reflect the interplay between these considerations and the technological and economic attributes of the infrastructure. What are the physical, technological, and economic characteristics of highways that determine whether they should be provided using public provision, PPPs, or privatization?

3.1 Physical and Economic Characteristics

Highway investments are large, sunk upfront, and long-lived. Interurban highways tend to be natural monopolies, while urban highways are usually part of a network. It follows that public intervention is justified, either to regulate tolls or to coordinate network planning and to oversee the intensive use of public space and rights-of-way. This typically rules out privatization, so that the choice for most highways is between a PPP and traditional provision.

Second, as mentioned in Section 1.4, highway deterioration depends mainly on usage, and it is highly nonlinear in axle weight. In addition, if a new road is not adequately maintained, it deteriorates slowly until quality falls dramatically. It is much more expensive to repair the road at this point than to perform routine maintenance on it. Thus, without continuous maintenance, road quality suffers.

Third, highways are excludable and, to the extent that congestion is an issue, rival. This implies that tolls can be used to finance them and manage congestion.

Finally, a key characteristic of highways is that, for all practical purposes, services are contractible, that is, independent third parties can specify and verify quality standards at a low cost. Box 3.1 illustrates this point by describing a PPP contract for a network of roads between a forestry company and a private firm.

Box 3.1 *Contractible highway services[1]*

A forestry company in Latin America subcontracted the construction and maintenance of a 60-kilometer road network of six roads for heavy trucks within its forests.

The life of the contract was for five years or until a predetermined volume of lumber was carried on the network, whichever occurred first. The payment schedule specified a unit price per kilometer (P), 24 percent of which was to be paid on completion of the road's foundation, 36 percent on completion of the road, and the remaining 40 percent in 60 monthly installments. Should the contract end in month $m < 60$, there would be a final payment of $0.292(60 - m)P$.

The 10-page contract specifies building standards such as width and thickness of asphalt. Each kilometer of every road is classified into one of the following three states at any point in time: damaged (when the damaged area is less than 30 square meters of the asphalt cover per kilometer); collapsed (if there is more damage than in the damaged category); or optimal (if the road is neither collapsed nor damaged).

Next, the contract defines the road as a whole to be collapsed if traffic is interrupted or if it has at least one collapsed kilometer, and this definition is used to specify service standard requirements. A damaged kilometer must be repaired within seven days or the concessionaire receives no monthly payment for that kilometer. A collapsed road must be repaired to the damaged state within 24 hours, or the concessionaire will receive no monthly payment for the entire road and it forfeits performance bonds. ∎

3.2 When Are PPPs Appropriate for Highways?

Whether a PPP is the best choice depends on the physical characteristics of roads, in particular the peculiar way they deteriorate and the fact that highway services are contractible. Incentives for allocating resources for routine maintenance are low under traditional provision because it may take years for the effects of insufficient maintenance to emerge, so that the political consequences of worsening quality may well fall on the next administration. Moreover, repairs after the road deteriorates have political visibility,

---

[1] Based on a private contract we had access to on condition of not identifying the project.

providing another incentive to lower the allocation of resources to routine maintenance. This leads to a stop-and-go approach to highway maintenance in most developing and some developed countries, which raises maintenance costs considerably (to triple the cost of timely maintenance, according to some estimates) and lowers average quality.

If the PPP contract specifies quality standards, the concessionaire has strong incentives to maintain the road. Because it is much more expensive to repair a severely damaged road than to perform routine maintenance, the concessionaire will choose to perform routine maintenance on a regular basis (at least before the approach of the end of the contract). This also provides incentives for the concessionaire to design the project to minimize life-cycle costs while maintaining the quality standards specified in the contract. It follows that if property rights in a country are protected, so that firms do not require a significant premium to enter a contractual relation in which they sink a large investment repaid over a relatively long period, then PPPs are the preferred organizational form for highways. If PPPs are not feasible, delegating supervision of maintenance to local authorities may lead to significant improvements (see Box 3.2 for two examples).

Box 3.2 *Improving maintenance under traditional provision*[2]

In Peru in 1996, only 6 percent of the 28,556 kilometers in the rural road network assigned to the newly created Rural Road Program (PROVIAS-Rural) was in good condition. The aim of the program was to substitute continuous maintenance for the past cycle of construction, no maintenance, and reconstruction. The program chose to use labor-based techniques, in which microenterprises were assigned a stretch of 25 kilometers of road (on average), with the requirement that the road be usable year round. The work consisted of filling potholes, clearing drains and culverts, and cutting vegetation using hand tools and wheelbarrows. The microenterprises received a fixed payment per kilometer per year.[3] The microenterprises were initially set up by PROVIAS-Rural, which hoped people would eventually set up the businesses on their own. The program had a very positive impact, with a large increase in the fraction of the road network kept in good state.

In 2002 PROVIAS-Rural established a decentralization program to increase the sustainability of the program by including local funding and, eventually, provincial-level management. The municipalities were required to finance 40 percent of program costs by deducting the resources from the Common Municipal Fund, funded by the central government. Given the centralized nature of the municipal fund, it is not clear that the incentives were appropriate.

---

[2] Based on Quispe and Cartier (2003).
[3] The payment scheme was later changed to a system of differentiated payments based on service level and difficulty (slopes, existing drainage works, rainfall, and so forth).

Another example is found in francophone Africa, where a number of countries have set up project implementation agencies (usually known by their French acronym, AGETIP, or *Agence d'exécution des travaux d'intérêt public contre le sous-emploi*). These agencies are essentially independent, decentralized, and private nonprofit organizations operating with their own staff. They carry out the preliminary engineering, request bids, and manage projects on behalf of the local governments, which keep the right to select projects and pay for them. The agencies are governed by an independent board, and the staff is competitively hired and paid market wages.

AGETIPs seem to be an attractive alternative, combining scale economies with decentralization. They have worked in poor countries, in particular in Senegal. As Heggie and Vickers (1998) report, they routinely obtain unit prices that are between 5 percent and 40 percent lower than those obtained by governments. ▪

3.3 How to Implement PPPs

A central economic characteristic to be heeded when designing the contract for a highway PPP is that there is large, mainly exogenous demand risk. This risk arises because demand forecasts are unreliable. Demand forecasts are based on estimates of future growth of the overall economy, adjusted for deviations in the region in which the project is located. An increase or decrease in the rate of growth of demand by 1 percent or 2 percent over a long period can have huge effects on the project's returns. Demand forecasts also depend on estimates of the macroeconomic cycle, which are tied to the aggregate performance of the economy, and estimates of microeconomic conditions, which reflect local demand fluctuations.

For example, both sources of demand risk have been important in Chile, even during the most stable decade in the country's recent economic history. Table 3.1 shows the increase in the number of motor vehicles paying tolls in 1986–1995 on three of the main toll roads near Santiago.[4] Because tolls remained approximately constant (in real terms) during this period, fluctuations in growth rates are mainly due to demand fluctuations. Macroeconomic risk is reflected, for example, in the fact that vehicle flows grew much faster in 1988 than in 1990. There is also microeconomic risk, because the changes in vehicle flow growth rates in different tollbooths are not correlated and exhibit sizable fluctuations around the annual average.

---

[4] The rates correspond to the growth in the flow of vehicles from one year to the next. For example, the vehicle flow through the Angostura tollbooth grew 8.8 percent between 1986 and 1987. These flows are representative, covering the three busiest highways near Santiago.

Table 3.1. *Demand uncertainty in Chilean toll roads: Percentage increase*

Toll road	1986	1987	1988	1989	1990	1991	1992	1993	1994
Angostura	8.8	15.0	11.7	4,5	8.7	12.4	6.7	7.8	9.4
Zapata	21.5	14.4	13.1	8.1	7.2	5.2	2.9	3.9	4.9
Lampa	3.8	13.4	15.9	8.9	6.8	18.0	8.8	16.2	12.5

Demand risk may also stem from uncertainty about changes in the income elasticity of demand for motor vehicles and uncertainty about the toll rate elasticity. Either of these sources of risk may throw off demand forecasts, which are usually inaccurate in the short term (three to five years) and all but useless in the long term.

Demand forecasts can be very imprecise even in industrialized countries, where the quantity and quality of information is far better. For example, the Dulles Greenway is a 14-mile (22.5 km) road joining Leesburg, Virginia, with Dulles airport in the Washington, DC area. When the concession was granted in the mid-1990s, two consulting companies independently fore-cast a ridership of 35,000 vehicles a day if the toll was set at $1.75. Actual traffic turned out to be 8,500 vehicles a day, partly because consultants underestimated how much users dislike paying tolls and partly because they did not take into account the State of Virginia's widening of the con-gested and toll-free Route 7, which serves the same users. While in this case demand risk was partly policy related, it was beyond the firm's control and thus exogenous.

Large demand risk implies that risk sharing is key in a PPP contract. Given that opportunistic renegotiations have been a major problem under PPPs, governments should make the firm bear little demand risk. This will provide fewer excuses to renegotiate the contract when demand is low. This also takes care of the fact that agency problems make it difficult for firms to unload the demand risk they are forced to bear.

Despite the high demand uncertainty highway concessions face, it is often the case that tolls will eventually pay for the project, with the ques-tion being how long it will take. For example, even though demand for the Dulles Greenway initially proved much lower than expected, accumulated toll revenue would have eventually paid for capital and operating expenses. For highways that will eventually pay for themselves, a particular type of flexible-term contract, known as a present-value-of-revenue (PVR) con-tract, is attractive. Under a PVR contract, the regulator sets the discount rate and toll schedule, and firms bid the present value of toll revenue they desire. The firm that makes the lowest bid wins, and the contract term lasts until the winning firm collects the toll revenue it asked for.

One advantage of a PVR contract is that it reduces risk: when demand is lower than expected, the franchise period is longer, while the period is shorter if demand is unexpectedly high. Assuming that the project is profitable in the long run so that repayment eventually occurs, all demand risk has been eliminated. Compared with fixed-term concessions, this reduces the risk premium demanded by the firm (for example, by an amount equal to one-third of the upfront investment in the case considered by Engel, Fischer, and Galetovic, 2001, and by an even larger amount in the case considered in Albalate and Bel, 2009). This should attract investors at lower discount rates than traditional fixed-term Demsetz franchises. Annual user fee revenues are the same under both franchises, but the franchise term is variable under PVR. If demand is low, the franchise holder of a fixed-term contract may default; in contrast, a PVR concession is extended until user fee revenue equals the bid, which makes default less probable. The PVR bondholders do not know when they will be repaid, but that is less costly than not being paid at all. PVR schemes also reduce the need for guarantees because the risk to investors is much smaller. Furthermore, the winner's curse is less likely with smaller demand risk and bids become more cost oriented (Tirole, 1997).

England was probably the first country to use a contract with some of the characteristics of a PVR. The Queen Elizabeth II Bridge on the Thames River, a 450-meter-long bridge connecting Dartford in the south and Thurrock in the north, was given in concession for a variable term. The construction was financed with subordinated debt issued by insurance companies, with repayment only after operating expenses were met. There was no equity in the project because there was no risk involved. The bridge opened in 1991 and the franchise lasted until toll collections paid off the debt issued to finance the bridge, which occurred in March 2002, almost 10 years before the maximum franchise period of 20 years. The special purpose vehicle (SPV) in charge of the concession was liquidated and the government began collecting tolls, now referred to as *charges*. The Second Severn Crossing on the Severn Estuary, which opened in 1996, also used a PVR-type contract. The contract stipulated a term of 30 years or until the concessionaire collected £995,830,000, expressed in July 1989 prices, whichever occurs first. In June 2010 the National Assembly of Wales forecast that the concession would end between 2016 and 2017.

Chile was the first country to use an outright PVR auction (see Box 3.3), while Colombia ran a flexible-term auction a couple of years earlier, in which firms bid on total income, without discounting. PVR auctions became the standard for auctioning highway PPPs in Chile in 2008: seven highway PPPs have been auctioned using this contract, with winning bids adding up to close to $2 billion (U.S. billion) (see Chapter 2 for details). Portugal also used a flexible-term contract in one important highway concession.

Box 3.3 *The first PVR auction*

The Route 68 concession, joining Santiago with Valparaíso and Viña del Mar, was auctioned in February 1998. It was the first road franchise ever awarded through a PVR auction. The Route 68 concession contemplated major improvements and extensions of the 130-kilometer highway and the construction of three new tunnels. Five firms bid in the auction, one of which was disqualified on technical grounds. For the first time in the Chilean concession program, minimum traffic guarantees were not given away, but were a costly option. That the government's pricing of guarantees was not far off the mark can be inferred from the fact that two of the bidders chose to buy a guarantee, while the winner declined. Bidders could choose between two rates to discount their annual incomes: either a fixed (real) rate of 6.5 percent or a variable (real) rate given by the average rate in the Chilean financial system for operations between 90 and 365 days. A 4 percent risk premium was added to both discount rates. Three firms, including the winner, chose the option with a fixed discount rate. Somewhat surprising, the present value of revenue demanded by the winner turned out to be below construction and maintenance costs estimated by the Ministry of Public Works (MOP): the winner bid $374 million (U.S. million), while MOP estimated costs to be $379 million. One possible explanation for this outcome is that the regulator set the risk premium (and hence the discount rate) too high, neglecting the fact that PVR auctions substantially reduce the risk faced by the franchise holder. A return on capital in the 10–20 percent range is obtained with a more reasonable risk premium (in the 1–2 percent range). ∎

A second advantage of PVR contracts is that they provide a natural fair compensation should the PWA decide to terminate the franchise early. The contract need only include a clause allowing the PWA to buy out the franchise by paying the difference between the winning bid and the discounted value of collected toll revenue at the time of repurchase (minus a simple estimate of savings in maintenance and operating expenditures due to early termination). No such simple compensation is available if the franchised term is fixed.[5]

---

[5] The MOP used a PVR contract because the fair compensation is straightforward should the ministry decide to terminate the franchise early. This feature of PVR schemes is

Third, the flexibility incorporated into PVR contracts is convenient for urban highways. Setting the appropriate ex ante toll for these projects is a complex task. Unless traffic forecasters are unusually fortunate in their estimates, the resulting tolls are likely to be incorrect – sometimes so low that they create congestion or possibly so high that the highway is underutilized. In a PVR franchise, the regulator could set tolls efficiently to alleviate congestion, without distorting the incentives of the concessionaire (care must be taken to ensure that the tolls generate sufficient revenue to pay for initial capital expenditures).

Fourth, a PVR contract also reduces the likelihood of bad faith renegotiations. Traditional fixed-term infrastructure contracts are often renegotiated by extending the length of the concession, increasing user fees, or providing a government transfer (or some combination thereof). Extending the concession term in a PVR contract is not possible because, by definition, the term is variable. Increasing user fees is ineffective because it shortens the concession term without increasing overall income. Government transfers are not impossible, but they should be harder to explain to the public because the concessionaire cannot claim that it will receive less user fee revenue than it expected. Furthermore, to the extent that firms are more likely to act opportunistically under financial duress, PVR contracts reduce firms' incentives to lobby for renegotiations, because scenarios with losses for the firm are less likely.

While PVR contracts facilitate good faith renegotiations, deter bad faith renegotiations, reduce demand risk, and mitigate the winner's curse, the incentives to attract demand are weak because any action that increases demand shortens the contract term. Projects earn their income regardless of efforts by the concessionaire. In contrast, demand-increasing investments are more attractive under fixed-term franchises. This suggests that the PVR method is applicable when service quality is contractible and demand for the infrastructure is inelastic to the actions of the concessionaire, that is, when demand is mainly exogenous.

Infrastructure provided under a PPP often includes ancillary services that can be an important revenue source if properly managed, for example, stores and restaurants at an airport or gas stations along highways. A

---

relevant because the MOP estimates that at some point before the franchise ends, demand may have increased sufficiently to justify a substantial upgrade of the La Dormida highway, which competes with some sections of Route 68. Thus, the contract allows the MOP to buy back the franchise at any moment after the twelfth year of the franchise, paying the difference between the winning bid and the revenue already received, minus a simple estimate of savings in maintenance and operating costs due to early termination.

straightforward extension of the PVR contract can give adequate incentives to provide these ancillary services. While the concessionaire bids her desired PVR from user fees for the franchised infrastructure, she is free to exploit the ancillary services, either directly or by subcontracting them as the landlord of a shopping mall. It can be shown that rents from the ancillary services are competed away in the auction and that the concessionaire has incentives to maximize the profits from these services. At the same time, because the flow of customers is largely exogenous (they are attracted by the highway or the airport, not by the ancillary services), a variable term reduces exogenous demand risk for these services as well.

Finally, as mentioned earlier in the case of the United Kingdom's PFI, payments to contractors under a PPP typically do not begin until the building is completed. This provides incentives for finishing the project on time under a fixed-term contract. Similar incentives exist under a PVR contract if revenues are discounted to the date the building is completed.

Summing up, highways, port infrastructure, water reservoirs, and airport runways are natural candidates for PVR auctions because incentives to increase demand are not relevant.[6]

3.4 Conclusion

Overall, among projects that fit our definition of PPP (see Section 1.2), the amounts spent on highways are the most important. Highways have large upfront sunk costs and face uncertain demand. Poor maintenance under public provision is also common. For these projects, the main advantage of PPPs lies in providing good routine maintenance that keeps road quality at a high standard. Moreover, roads can be tolled electronically, so they generate revenue to help defray their costs (as opposed to availability payments).

The big issue with roads is that demand has large exogenous uncertainty over the life of the PPP contract and this imposes severe risks on investors who recover their expenses through toll revenues. In several dimensions relevant for roads, a type of contract known as PVR offers substantial benefits and solves the demand uncertainty problem. The advantage of PVR stems from having the franchise holder reveal the net present value of toll revenue that makes the project attractive, and from including a demand-contingent franchise term that ensures that this net present value is collected.

[6]   We mean basic port infrastructure, excluding equipment.

Bibliographic Notes

Charging users for using roads is, of course, an old idea, but recent technological advances have made it possible with substantially reduced toll collection costs. Small and Verhoef (2007) present a comprehensive survey of the field. The paper by Tsekeris and Voss (2009) contains a useful discussion of electronic tolling around the world. Small (2010) summarizes the economic issues raised by the private provision of highways. Small, Winston, and Evans (1989) is the classic source on road economics and efficient highway policy. They also explain the causes of road deterioration and optimal maintenance policies.

Auctions are the natural way of allocating a highway concession. The idea of competition for the field substituting for competition in the field can be traced back to Chadwick (1859) and was popularized by Demsetz (1968). See also Stigler (1968), Posner (1972), Riordan and Sappington (1987), Spulber (1989, Chapter 9), Laffont and Tirole (1993, chapters 7 and 8), and Harstad and Crew (1999) for papers within this tradition, and Williamson (1976, 1985) for a criticism.

Highway auctions with flexible terms were first analyzed in Engel, Fischer, and Galetovic (1996). Engel, Fischer, and Galetovic (2001) showed that PVR auctions are optimal under a self-financing constraint while Engel, Fischer, and Galetovic (2013) showed that a two-threshold auction is optimal when roads need subsidies. Flexible-term contracts are also analyzed in Nombela and de Rus (2004). Evidence of the winner's curse in highway auctions is found in Athias and Nuñez (2008, 2009).

A recent literature studies how the type of auction affects tolling and investment decisions: see Verhoef (2007, 2008), Ubbels and Verhoef (2008), and Chen and Subprasom (2007).

4

Incentives

This chapter studies the effect of PPPs on incentives. We compare PPPs with public provision and outright privatization, in terms of providing satisfactory service quality at a reasonable cost. As discussed earlier, the defects of public provision of infrastructure include white elephants and pork-barrel earmarks, lack of transparency in public work contracts, deficient maintenance and service quality, and even corruption. When the current trend of PPPs began some 20 years ago, its proponents believed that private participation in infrastructure alone would improve on these sorry results. Since then, PPPs have been used to provide traditional public infrastructure such as roads, bridges, tunnels, airports, and seaports, as well as complex infrastructure facilities such as schools, hospitals, prisons, and information technology. In light of this experience, the initial enthusiasm looks somewhat naïve: PPPs are one possible organizational form, and the appropriate organizational form depends both on the institutional and financial environment and on the characteristics of the project.

This chapter is divided into two parts. In the first, we study the project characteristics that make PPPs the preferred organizational arrangement. The second part examines alternative risk allocations between the government, private firms, and users of the infrastructure to see how they affect incentives in PPPs. In the first section, we assume a benevolent and efficient government that does not suffer any of the normal failures of real governments. This assumption is unrealistic, but it allows us to isolate the effects of the economic environment (e.g., whether returns to scale are increasing, constant, or decreasing) and of organizational form on incentives. In the remainder of this book, we make more realistic assumptions about governments.

4.1 When Do PPPs Work?

The literature identifies two distinguishing characteristics of PPPs that differentiate them from other forms of public service provision. First, a PPP is an intertemporal contract between the government and a private firm that bundles finance, construction, maintenance, and operations for a limited term. Bundling differentiates a PPP contract from public provision, in which the government selects a firm with the sole purpose of building an infrastructure facility, and the term limit differentiates PPPs from privatization. Second, during the PPP contract, the private firm has a large measure of freedom to manage the infrastructure. This implies that PPPs are akin to privatization in terms of incentives and control rights. These characteristics set up a basic trade-off: other things equal, PPP-induced bundling stimulates investments and other actions that reduce life-cycle costs and other costs more generally, but this cost cutting may occur at the expense of service quality and user welfare (we refer to this trade-off as *Hart's trade-off*). Thus, PPPs may or may not be the best alternative depending on project characteristics. Table 4.1 summarizes how project characteristics should influence the choice among privatization, PPPs, and public provision.

Privatization is possible only if user fees can be charged for the infrastructure services.[1] If the good or service is produced under constant or decreasing returns to scale, elementary economics proves that the optimal organizational form is privatization plus price deregulation, that is, market liberalization. Private ownership and competition induce the optimal amount of life-cycle cost savings and solve the trade-off between cost cutting and quality because competitive firms internalize consumer surplus – there is no need to impose service standards. Other cases require the government to establish and enforce technical rules, such as interconnection rules in mobile telephony. Perfect competition does not necessarily follow from liberalization, but competition policy can be left to competition authorities, as in other sectors.

When there are increasing returns and the industry is a natural monopoly, tariff regulation is necessary. This is the case of utilities, including water, electricity, and gas distribution. In general, regulated monopolies face the same cost-quality trade-off as PPPs, but there is sufficient experience

---

[1] Vouchers or direct subsidies could substitute for user fees in principle, but they seldom do in practice, except perhaps in education. This requires a well-defined and inelastic demand.

Table 4.1. *The economic environment and the choice of organizational form*

Environment			Organizational form
Increasing returns	Fees possible	Quality contractible	
No	Yes	Yes/No	Liberalization and privatization
Yes/No	No	Yes	PPP
Yes/No	No	No	PPP or conventional (Hart's trade-off)
Yes	Yes	Yes	Regulated privatization or PPP (planning-efficiency trade-off)
Yes	Yes	No	Regulated privatization or conventional (Hart's trade-off)

with tariff setting and establishing mechanisms for maintaining firms' incentives.

Neither market liberalization nor regulated privatization can work if the project is not excludable (as was the case of small roads until recently) or when society prefers not to charge users (for example, health services in countries with universal health care). Less obviously, PPPs have advantages when expansion requires network planning or when the scope of planning goes beyond a single project or area. Yet in the case of various utilities, planning issues are local and therefore compatible with privatization. For example, in the case of utilities like water or electricity distributors, which are characterized by local economies of density, facility planning does not require coordination across geographic areas and is best done by the firm. If the benefits of control rights increase with the duration of ownership, which is likely, privatization should be preferred over PPPs.

Container ports represent an example where planning issues often rule out privatization. The basic infrastructure required for a port (such as channels, protective works, and sea locks) and the infrastructure for access by road or train have to be planned before the port can operate. Container ports can be divided into independent terminals because the efficient scale of a container terminal is in the order of one million TEUs/year, which is much smaller than the scale of a large container port.[2] However, the basic port

---

[2] TEU is the acronym for a 20-foot equivalent unit, a unit of cargo capacity equivalent to a 20-foot-long shipping container. Megaports such as Singapore, Hong Kong, and Shanghai handle more than 20 million TEUs every year using several terminals operated by different specialized firms.

infrastructure cannot be easily allocated to particular users and is basically indivisible. The usual practice is to have a state-owned port authority, which acts as a landlord, does the long-term planning for the whole port, and has the authority to decide on future expansions. Terminals, by contrast, are operated by different firms, each with a concession contract that lasts for 20 or 30 years. If independent private firms owned the terminals indefinitely, it would be difficult to get them to coordinate when port expansion required new terminals or the physical modification of a terminal. Even worse, incumbents would try to block the entry of new terminals. However, if the port were privatized as a single unit, the owner would enjoy monopoly power and would underinvest in new container terminals. While tariffs could be regulated, competition among terminals has been shown to lead to better results than regulation.

Most transportation infrastructure – including roads, tunnels, bridges, seaports, airports, and railways – are part of networks, which need long-term planning by a public authority. To a large extent, objective service standards can be defined and enforced in these cases, so that quality is contractible. This makes PPPs the adequate organizational form because once service standards are set, the firm can be left free to choose the optimal combination of inputs that minimizes costs. This is so regardless of the funding source for the project. If the infrastructure can be financed with user fees, PPPs are better than privatization; if they must be financed by government transfers, then PPPs dominate public provision.

The choice is not so clear-cut when quality is not contractible, because a trade-off between cost cutting and service quality emerges. It is sometimes possible to regulate service quality indirectly by specifying amounts and quality of inputs. However, given the inputs required by the government, bundling implies that the firm will choose the profit-maximizing combination of cost-saving and quality-reducing investment, subject to the constraints imposed by the government. Regulating service quality thus requires a close relationship between input and service quality. Otherwise, the public authority must retain at least some control and discretion over managerial decisions. This weakens the private party's control rights, introduces rigidity in its choices, and may even inhibit the firm from adopting new and better technologies. If the associated cost is sufficiently high, public provision is the preferred alternative.

Consider schools. Important aspects of primary and secondary education, about which parents and society care (such as moral values), are not contractible, because they cannot be measured with standardized tests. A variety of inputs can be specified (for example, the number of students per teacher, teacher seniority and degrees, and equipment), but they are only partially related to the overall quality of education. Even if specifying inputs helps to attain reasonable levels of educational quality, it may also limit innovative options that increase efficiency. For example, limiting the number of students per teacher may discourage expenditures on software that partly substitutes for in-classroom teaching or that extends the reach of gifted teachers.

To conclude, the decision between public provision and PPPs is not about the source of financing. PPPs can work with both user fees and subsidies, and public provision is not incompatible with user fees. Indeed, one of the main points of this book is that whether a PPP or public provision is better is a matter of relative productive and allocative efficiency – the source of the funds that finance the project is not the relevant issue.

Thus, PPPs emerge as the preferred alternative when quality is contractible and the scope of planning exceeds the scope of each project. If planning is best done at the level of each firm and if user fees can be charged, privatization is often a better choice. If quality is not contractible and is the main concern of public policy, then public provision is probably the appropriate organizational form.

4.2 Risk Allocation and Incentives in PPPs

Risk is one of the main themes in the PPP discussion. Risks in a PPP contract can be classified into seven different categories, which sometimes are related and overlap:[3] (i) construction risk, including design flaws, cost overruns, and delays; (ii) operation and maintenance (O&M) risk; (iii) performance risk, including the availability of the service or infrastructure and uncertainty about service quality more generally; (iv) residual value risk, mainly uncertainty about the value of the assets at the end of the PPP contract; (v) policy risk, ranging from macroeconomic uncertainty, which affects all sectors of the economy, to government actions that affect mainly the project (for example, building untolled alternative roads); (vi) demand risk, that is, uncertainty about the future rate of use of the infrastructure; (vii) financial risk, including interest rate and exchange rate fluctuations and any other factor affecting financing; and (viii) political risk, that is, the possibility of regulatory takings or plain expropriation.

---

[3]   See, for example, Cangiano, Hemming, and Ter-Minassian (2004); Hall (1998); Irwin (2007).

These risks must be distributed among the government, the private firm, and the users of the project. Irwin has clearly stated the appropriate principle: the contract should allocate risks and related rights so as to maximize project value, taking account of each party's ability to influence, anticipate, and absorb risk – and transaction costs (2007, p. 65). This is quite general, but it implies that controllable risks should be borne, at least in part, by the party best equipped to control them, as this creates incentives to be efficient. At the same time, exogenous risk should be shifted to the party best endowed to bear or diversify it (see Chapter 5). Under public provision, taxpayers bear most of these risks.[4] The main exception is availability and service quality risks, which only affect users. Because taxpayers rarely influence governments' decisions, and many bureaucrats respond to users' concerns only imperfectly or when forced by political pressures, presumably there is a large potential for efficiency gains in using PPPs.

Consider first construction risk. The time to completion and the cost of building often exceed initial projections, and these factors usually can only be controlled by the builder. The private firm should therefore bear these risks (perhaps with the exception of delays caused by disputes about the application of eminent domain).[5] Similarly, because design and diligence during construction influence the availability of the facility, O&M costs, and service quality, these risks should also be borne by the private firm. If these risks are effectively transferred, then PPP arrangements should be substantially more efficient than public provision because under public provision these risks are borne by taxpayers and users rather than by those who design and build the project.

Bundling, control, and service standards are all required to ensure that these risks are effectively transferred to the private firm. For example, it is harder to make a firm accountable for service quality if it was not responsible for designing and building the facility (hence the importance of bundling) or if the firm has no control rights over investment and operational decisions (hence the importance of control, or ownership, rights). Similarly, without objective and measurable service standards, it is

---

[4] Contractors nominally bear construction risks, but in practice one of the shortcomings of public provision is endemic contract renegotiation, which effectively shifts the risks to taxpayers.

[5] When construction risk is excessive as a result of fundamental exogenous uncertainty, as in tunnels, the usual practice is to include cost-sharing agreements that are triggered when geological conditions are worse than expected. This creates moral hazard problems, but it may be the only option when uncertainty is great; otherwise, the risk premium the concessionaire charges to protect against tail risk is too large.

difficult to transfer service quality risk away from users of the facility and to the firm.

As Hall (1998) points out, the extent to which risks are transferred largely depends on the choice of payment mechanism. To create strong incentives to complete the project on time, the firms should only receive payments after the facility is in service. Similarly, payments that are contingent on the availability of the facility and on meeting service quality standards generate strong incentives for adequate maintenance and proper management. By contrast, payments that are independent of performance or, worse, that transfer high costs to taxpayers, reproduce the incentives of public provision.

Some of the risks on our list are controlled or even created by the government. As we have mentioned, one of the main advantages of PPPs is that the government retains planning authority and discretion. Because the residual value of PPP assets depends on government planning decisions (not to mention that most assets are project specific), it is reasonable to transfer that risk to the government. This is ensured when the private firm recovers its initial investment over the term of the contract and then transfers the residual value to the government. This principle suggests that the government should bear some policy risks so as to avoid moral hazard.

Policy risks can be classified, broadly speaking, into two categories. First, the government may implement policies that directly affect the project and have few other effects. For example, it may build or expand a road that competes with the tolled PPP or change the rules with the express purpose of expropriating the concessionaire. In general, the government should bear these policy risks to prevent it from behaving opportunistically. Second, actions by the government or congress may unintentionally affect the PPP. For example, devaluation may reduce a foreign firm's return or a change in environmental standards may require additional investments. In these cases, the government is not acting opportunistically, and the private firm is in the same position as any other private firm in the economy. Therefore, there is no reason for the government to bear this risk and compensate the PPP. This principle is routinely overlooked. For example, governments often grant foreign concessionaires insurance against devaluations. Not only does this discriminate against local investors, but it also discriminates against foreign firms in other sectors of the economy that must bear exchange rate risk. More generally, policy risks that do not target the project specifically and that affect most firms in the economy (for example, those caused by monetary policy) should be treated as exogenous and allocated according to general principles of risk diversification.

Perhaps the main exogenous risk in a PPP project is uncertainty about demand over the life of the contract. The general principle is that exogenous demand risk should be borne by the party best able to bear it. If the private firm assumes demand risk, taxpayers are in fact purchasing an insurance contract on an exogenous risk that they assume under public provision (we discuss this further in Chapter 5). As Hall (1998) notes, this is not cost effective. Demand forecasts are notoriously imprecise and changes in policy, which are unknown at the time of tendering, may radically affect the usage of the facility, yet there is little that the firm can do about it.[6] Moreover, facilities are largely planned by the government, not by the firm. In those cases, either a present-value-of-revenue contract or availability payments are the appropriate compensation scheme, depending on whether the main source of funds is user fees or government transfers.

The principle of transferring exogenous demand risk to the government admits one important exception. When user fees are a PPP's only source of remuneration, the willingness of private firms to bid for the contract is a market signal that demand is sufficient (at least in expectation). This introduces a market test that is usually absent in infrastructure services and that helps to avoid white elephants. If there are no bidders at an auction, this is a signal that the project is not privately profitable and therefore there is a risk that the project is a white elephant unless it has large positive externalities.

As in the case of demand risk, financial risk is largely outside the firm's control. This does not mean, however, that the government should bear interest rate or exchange rate risk. Other firms in the economy do not receive this favored treatment, and firms can choose among alternative capital structures. More generally, governments are not particularly efficient at providing and selling financial insurance. We discuss this issue at length in Chapter 5.

4.3 Unsolicited Proposals

It is often the case that a private party approaches the PWA with the idea for an infrastructure project. When the idea is good and does not belong to the set of projects under study by the PWA, the proponent should be remunerated in order to create incentives for the private sector to contribute additional worthy proposals. The question is how to structure a procedure such

---

[6] This is, for example, the case of highways, where the actions of the franchise holder have little effect on demand if contracted service levels are adequate and enforced; see Chapter 3.

that the private sector generates innovative ideas for infrastructure projects. This requires the development of mechanisms for compensating the private parties for their ideas without affecting the transparency and efficiency of PPP awards.[7] Countries that have developed systems for receiving unsolicited proposals must deal with large numbers of proposals, running into the hundreds in the cases of Chile, South Korea, and Taiwan. The PWA may contract with the proponent to develop the project as a PPP, but the lack of competition, the opaqueness, and the room it leaves for corruption have made this option unattractive.

The alternative is to design a clear-cut mechanism for remunerating innovative proposals. The first stage consists of approving or rejecting the unsolicited proposal, according to explicit guidelines (in particular, excluding obviousness). Once an unsolicited proposal is approved, there are various options for remunerating the proponent. In some countries the proponent has an advantage in the competitive auction for the project, which is transferable. Its bid is chosen if it is no more than, say, 5 or 10 percent off the best bid. In other countries, the proponent can match the best offer. The problem with these approaches is that the proponent's advantage may discourage further participation in the auction, leading to projects being awarded with little competition.

An additional problem with this approach is that the proposing firm will lobby for the development of the project. In the case of urban infrastructure projects, these pressures may interfere with urban planning. In Santiago, the El Salto-Kennedy tunnel was built and began to be used even though the exits of the tunnel into a congested sector of the city had not been defined at the time, worsening the existing congestion (see Bitrán and Villena, 2010).

The alternative, which we espouse, is to separate the proposal stage from the award stage. Each year, the PWA chooses a small number of proposals, and the selected proponents receive a fixed prize sufficiently appealing to attract good projects. The prize is paid by the PWA and reimbursed by the winner of the project once it is awarded under competitive conditions. This proposal gives incentives for competition in unsolicited proposals but does not alter the competitiveness and transparency of the award process.

4.4 Conclusion

This chapter analyzed the main reason for PPPs: the fact that bundling induces efficient behavior. The types of infrastructure projects that are best

---

[7] See Hodges and Dellacha (2007) for more details on unsolicited proposals.

provided under PPPs require that incentives to reduce costs do not reduce service quality, either because this is not in the best interests of the private firm or because quality standards can be enforced. Moreover, it must be the case that privatization is not a good option because it might interfere with long-term planning of infrastructure, as in the case of a road network or ports.

We also examined the general principles of risk allocation in PPPs and showed that risks under the control of the firm (construction and O&M risks) should, except for very specific exceptions, be borne by the concessionaire. This provides the appropriate incentives for cost-reducing efforts. Moreover, nonspecific government-induced risks (devaluation, for example), to which all local firms are subject, should also be borne by the concessionaire; otherwise it would receive special discriminatory treatment. However, exogenous demand risk should be borne by society, and this can be achieved by either PVR contracts in the case that user fees are an important component of revenue, or by availability contracts.

We concluded by examining how to deal with unsolicited proposals for infrastructure projects and proposed a scheme that attracts good projects from the public while avoiding the disadvantages of present schemes to reward firms that present those proposals.

Bibliographic Notes

As discussed in this chapter, PPPs lie between privatization and public provision. Several papers reexamine the role of government in the provision of goods and services, a theme of direct relevance for PPPs. On the theoretical side, Schmidt (1996a, 1996b) studies the pros and cons of privatization; Hart, Shleifer, and Vishny (1997) address the appropriate scope of government; and Besley and Ghatak (2001) examine how ownership matters in public good provision. King and Pitchford (2008) develop a taxonomy to determine who should own assets to provide public services.

Useful discussions about which goods and services should be produced by the government and which should be left to the market are provided by Daniels and Trebilcock (1996, 2000), Domberger and Jensen (1997), Gerrard (2001), Grout and Stevens (2003), Savas (2000), Shleifer (1998), and Starr (1988). See also the survey by Jensen and Stonecash (2005) on contracting out in the public sector.

Perhaps the most influential theoretical study of PPPs is by Hart (2003), who first applied the incomplete contracting approach to PPPs. This paper shows that PPPs work best when cost cutting is the main concern, but that they may induce poor quality. Bennet and Iossa (2006a) extend Hart's analysis in several directions and show that by transferring control rights, PPPs stimulate the unilateral implementation of cost-saving innovations. See also Bennet and Iossa (2006b) for a comparison of delegation in public contracts and in PPPs.

A second strand of the literature studies the agency costs of delegated public provision via PPPs; how contracts should be designed; and when bundling under PPPs improves incentives. Recent contributions include Bentz, Grout, and Halonen (2005), Martimort and Pouyet (2008), Iossa and Martimort (2012), and Auriol and Picard (2013).

An early and insightful discussion of the advantages and disadvantages of procurement via PPPs can be found in Hall (1998); see also Riess (2005). Value-for-money tests, which compare the costs of public procurement and PPPs, are analyzed by Grout (2003, 2005), Grout and Sonderegger (2006), and Engel and Galetovic (2012). Välilä (2005) discusses when PPPs are likely to save costs; see also Grimsey and Lewis (2005a).

Irwin (2007) offers a comprehensive treatment of risks in PPPs. Useful classifications of risks are found in Cangiano, Hemming, and Ter-Minassian (2004) and in Grimsey and Lewis (2002). See also the discussion in Dewatripont and Legros (2005). Iossa and Martimort (2012) and Engel, Fischer, and Galetovic (2013) analyze the optimal allocation of risks in PPP contracts.

5

Private Finance

The growth and spread of PPPs around the world is closely linked to the development of project finance, a financial technique that helps to borrow against the cash flow of a project that is legally and economically self-contained. The typical financial arrangement for a PPP, described in Section 5.1, has two characteristics. First, all financing is run through a so-called *special purpose vehicle* (SPV) – a stand-alone firm created for the sole purpose of developing the project. This firm is managed by the *sponsor*, who is an equity investor responsible for bidding, developing, and managing the project. Second, the sources of finance change over the project's life cycle. During construction, expenses are financed with sponsor equity (which may be complemented with bridge loans and subordinated or mezzanine debt) and bank loans. In some cases, the project may receive subsidies or minimum revenue guarantees from the government. Once the PPP project becomes operational, in many cases long-term bonds replace bank loans, and the sponsor's equity may be bought out by a facility operator or even by passive third-party investors, usually institutional investors.

The changing sources of finance match the evolving pattern of risks and incentives over the life cycle of PPP projects. Most changes to the specifications of such projects occur during construction. Yescombe notes that banks exercise control over all changes of the PPP contract and tightly constrain the project company's behavior (2007, p. 141). They are thus well suited for lending during construction. By contrast, bondholders only have control (through the bond covenants) over issues that may significantly affect the security of cash flows; they cannot monitor the details of borrower behavior because of transaction costs. Consequently, they are better suited to finance the project during its operational phase, when there are fewer unforeseen events such as major project modifications.

In the United States before the financial crisis of 2008–2009, PPP projects were financed with bonds issued at the time of contract closure. The project sponsors bought cash flow insurance from a monoline insurer. With this guarantee, credit rating agencies gave an investment grade classification to the project from the start. Thus, the monolines performed the monitoring role of banks during the construction phase. Because monolines defaulted on their obligations during the 2008–2009 crisis, this business model is unlikely to return in the foreseeable future.

Project finance may be appropriate for financing PPPs, but many argue that it is more expensive than public debt and thus represents a disadvantage for PPPs in comparison with public provision. Indeed, project finance rates are typically higher than rates on government debt. In Section 5.2, we analyze this argument by considering the various sources of risk. The most important of these is demand risk. Because PPPs involve large upfront investments, exogenous demand risk is an important concern of lenders when user fees are the main revenue source. If the government bears this exogenous demand risk, lenders will demand lower risk premiums. However, PPPs are charged higher rates than government debt even when projects are based on availability payments (which eliminate demand risk). In this case, the higher rate reflects the risk that the infrastructure will be unavailable at some point in the life of the contract, and reduced payments will be received to service the debt. Unavailability risk is also present under traditional provision, except that the risk falls on users. Finally, the risk associated with construction costs of a PPP is similar to the risk under a price-cap construction contract, which also provides strong incentives for cost reduction and thus may be efficient.

We suggest that the higher costs of project finance are due partly to faulty contract design and partly to the cost-cutting incentives embedded in PPPs. For a well-designed PPP contract, the higher cost of capital may well be the flip side of the efficiency advantage of PPPs vis-à-vis public provision.

5.1 Financial Arrangements in PPPs

The typical PPP infrastructure project involves a large initial upfront investment that is sunk, followed by operating and maintenance costs that are paid over the life of the project. Maintenance and operating costs are often a relatively small fraction of total costs in present value, and this fact determines several characteristics of PPP finance. Figure 5.1 shows the typical time profile of the financial flows of a PPP project. It assumes that the interest rate is 12 percent, revenues grow 5 percent each year, and debt payments

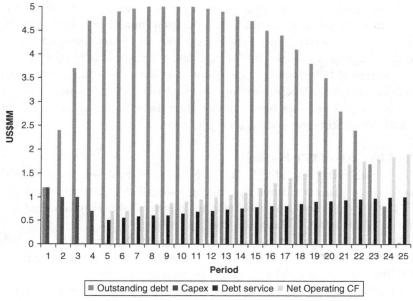

Figure 5.1. Time profile of financial flows.

grow 3.5 percent each year. Capital expenditures occur during the first four years. Revenues over the life of the project pay off the debt by year 25. After the initial capital expenditure, the main objectives of the project are to collect revenues, which are then disbursed to pay for outstanding debt, and to generate dividends for the equity holders.

Three additional economic characteristics of most PPP projects are important for understanding the choice of financial arrangements. First, PPP projects are usually large enough to require independent management, especially during construction and frequently also during the operational phase. Moreover, there are few synergies to be realized by building or operating two or more large PPP projects together (note that in the case of small projects, such as schools, bundling may be efficient). For instance, the projects may be located far apart, and efficient scale is site specific. Moreover, project assets are illiquid and have little value if the project fails.

Second, most of the production processes, during both construction and operation, are subcontracted. Hence, any scale and scope economies are internalized by specialized service providers, such as construction companies, maintenance contractors, and toll collectors. Moreover, from the lender's point of view, it shifts risks to the subcontractors, which, unlike the SPV, have resources.

Third, as we discussed in Chapter 4, when services are contractible, it is efficient to bundle construction and operation. Bundling forces investors to internalize operating and maintenance costs and generates incentives to design the project so that it minimizes life-cycle costs. Finally, when a firm is in charge of long-term operations and maintenance, it has incentives to maintain the infrastructure on an ongoing basis. Routine maintenance is less costly and provides better service than the stop-and-go approach to maintenance common under public provision.

The Life Cycle of PPP Finance

The growth and spread of PPPs is closely linked to the development of project finance.[1] This is ensured by creating a so-called special purpose vehicle (SPV), which does not undertake any business other than building and operating the project (Yescombe, 2002, p. 318).

As mentioned earlier, before the bidding for the project takes place, an SPV is set up by a sponsor, who is the equity investor responsible for bidding, developing, and managing the project. The sponsor is the residual claimant and is essential to the success of the project. This means that lenders will carefully examine the characteristics of the sponsor before committing resources. Sponsors can be operational or financial. An operational sponsor belongs to the industry and will secure business for itself as a subcontractor. The Queen Elizabeth II Bridge over the Dartford River in the United Kingdom is an example of an operational sponsor: the construction division of Trafalgar House PLC organized local landowners plus an investment bank and presented an initial proposal to the government, which the Department of Transport ultimately approved (Levy, 1996). A financial sponsor is primarily interested in the financial arrangements for the project. The main sponsor of the Dulles Greenway project in Virginia was a family-owned investment company, Toll Road Investors Partnership II, which held 57 percent of project equity (see Levy, 1996).

Although the SPV remains active throughout the project until the assets revert to the government, there is a clear demarcation between financing during the construction phase and financing during the operational phase. This is shown in Figure 5.2 for a user fee-financed project. During construction, sponsor equity is combined with bank loans and, sometimes, government grants in money or kind. In the case of projects that derive their revenues from user fees, the initial contribution to investment might be supplemented with government subsidies if the project revenues

---

[1] See Yescombe (2007) for a detailed analysis.

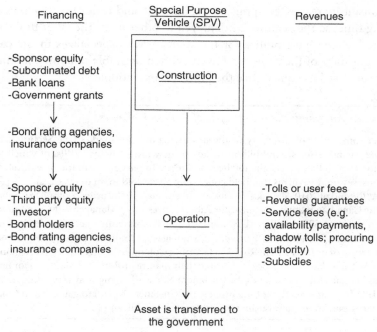

Figure 5.2. The financial life cycle of a PPP.

are insufficient. After completion of the construction stage and success-ful operation, bondholders replace bank lenders as the primary creditors. Bond finance is associated with two additional entities: rating agencies and insurance companies. As mentioned earlier, when the PPP project becomes operational, the sponsor's equity may be bought out by a facility operator or even by passive third-party investors, usually pension or mutual funds. Bondholders, of course, have priority over the project's cash flow.

Initial sponsors supply the project's original equity, and they are typically required to keep a fraction until the project is operational. None of these requirements were met by the U.S. 63–20 tax-exempt PPP projects that failed in the United States (see Section 2.3). Holding equity provides incentives for sponsors during the design and construction phases, for example, to make investments that minimize life-cycle costs. They are sometimes required to keep a fraction of equity until the end of the PPP contract, without the option of an equity transfer, in an effort to provide longer-term incentives. This may be justified when investments that lead to significant cost reduc-tion or efficiency gains during the operational phase cannot be verified by prospective buyers. Otherwise, it is expensive for the initial sponsor for two reasons: it increases the sponsor's capital cost, and it ties up resources for a long time, so they cannot be deployed to other uses. The latter limits the future business possibilities for the sponsor, who specializes in the early building stage of the project. Thus, it is often desirable to allow the initial sponsor to sell its equity once the project is operational.

Box 5.1 *An example of the life cycle of PPPs in highways*

After some years of inactivity in the infrastructure PPP market (see Section 2.2), Chile has plans for several billion dollars in new infrastructure PPPs, of which $2 billion (U.S. billion) have already been awarded. To participate in the new developments, several PPP firms that held concessions have sold them to raise cash.

At the end of 2010, Skanska sold its 50 percent share in the urban Autopista Central to the Canadian institutional investor Alberta Investment Management Corporation for a profit of $731 million (U.S. million) and almost immediately made the best offer, winning a highway PPP project in Antofagasta.[2] Another operator, Cintra, sold 60 percent of its five PPPs in Ruta 5 to ISA from Colombia.[3] Currently OHL, Acciona, and ACS are also in the process of selling their mature projects in order to go for new ones.[4] Finally, the controller of the Costanera Norte urban highway is planning to do an IPO (selling a fraction of the property of Costanera Norte) to gather fresh funds to participate in the new business opportunities in Chilean PPPs.[5] ∎

As mentioned earlier, the life cycle of PPP finance and the change in the financing source is determined by the different incentive problems faced during the two stages of the PPP, namely, the construction and operational phases. Construction is subject to substantial uncertainty and major design changes, and its costs depend crucially on the diligence of the sponsor and the building contractor. This creates ample scope for moral hazard during this stage. Banks perform a monitoring role that can mitigate moral hazard by exercising tight control over changes to the project's contract and by scrutinizing the behavior of the SPV and its contractors (Tirole, 2006; Yescombe, 2007). To control behavior, banks disburse funds gradually as project stages are completed. Risk falls abruptly once the project is completed and initial demand uncertainty is revealed, after which risk is limited

---

[2] "Sueca Skanska vende participación en Autopista Central a inversionista canadiense," *El Mercurio*, December 29, 2010.

[3] "Cintra vende el 60% de su filial chilena a la colombiana ISA por casi US$ 300 millones," *El Mercurio*, September 16, 2010.

[4] "Tres grandes concesionarias españolas ponen a la venta sus principales carreteras en Chile," *El Mercurio*, March 4, 2011.

[5] "Matriz de Costanera Norte prevé abrirse a la bolsa chilena para abordar nuevas inversiones," *El Mercurio*, March 16, 2011.

only to events that may affect the cash flows from the project. This is suitable for bond finance because bondholders care only about events that significantly affect the security of the cash flows underpinning repayment, and thus they are not directly involved in management or in control of the PPP. As mentioned earlier, this risk profile is attractive for institutional and other passive investors, who by statutes can invest only small amounts of their funds during the initial stages of a PPP because of the high risk.

Financial contracts must address a number of incentive problems, which in the case of PPPs can be traced back to the contracts made by the SPV. Next we examine these contracts and the role of various agents.

The Web of Contracts of an SPV

The SPV lies at the center of a web of contracts, as illustrated in Figure 5.3. These include contracts with the procuring authority (usually the local or central government), with users of the services provided by the PPP, with building and operations contractors, and with the investors and financiers of the project. Each of these contracts is a potential source of conflict that may endanger debt holders. The success of the SPV in dealing with these conflicts depends on two factors: the quality of the legal institutions and laws on which the web of contracts rests and how the particulars of each relationship and contract affect risk perceptions by debt holders.

The project is intended to provide a service to users, but the fundamental contracting parties are the SPV and the procuring authority, which enforces the PPP contract and represents future users. Because contracts give at least some discretion to the procuring authority, cash flows and even the continuation of the concession may depend on the authority's decisions. Thus, ambiguous service standards and defective conflict resolution mechanisms increase risk. In addition, user fees will be at risk if the political authority is tempted to buy support or votes by lowering service fees either directly or by postponing inflation adjustments in so-called regulatory takings. Similarly, if a substantial fraction of the SPV's revenues are derived from payments by the procuring authority, these payments depend on the ability (or desire) of the government to fulfill its obligations. It follows that the governance structure of the procuring authority, its degree of independence, and the financial condition of the government affect the level of risk debt holders perceive.

Consider next the relationship of the SPV with construction firms and with operations and maintenance contractors. Many PPP projects involve complex engineering. Unexpected events are likely to arise in complex projects, and it becomes difficult to replace the building contractor. In

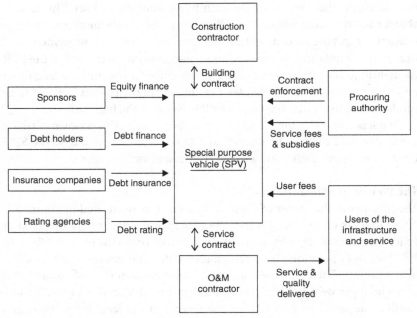

Figure 5.3. Web of contracts of an SPV.

these cases, the experience and reputation of the contractor are central to the project's success. The contractor's financial strength is also important because it determines the ability to credibly bear cost overruns without having to renegotiate the contract. The operational phase is less complex, but revenue flows depend on the fulfillment of the contracted service and quality standards, which, in turn, depends on the operations and maintenance contractor. Consequently, the experience and financial strength of the contractor concern debt holders. Debt holders also care about the type of risk-sharing agreements between the SPV and the contractors. Cost-plus contracts, which shift cost shocks to the SPV, are riskier than fixed-price contracts from their perspective.

Finally, debt holders care about the incentives of the sponsor, who provides around 30 percent of the funding in the typical highway PPP project (much less in PFI projects in the United Kingdom). This large chunk of equity has the lowest priority in the cash flow cascade, and it is typically committed by the sponsor (of course the equity owner or sponsor may change) until the project is operational or sometimes for the life of the PPP contract. Providers of funds worry about the financial strength and experience of sponsors, particularly during the construction and ramp-up phases of complex transportation projects. They value previous successful experience in the industry and technical prowess, and they look for evidence that the sponsor is committed to the project, financially and in terms of time and reputation. Lobbying ability with the procuring authority and its political taskmasters is also considered favorably at this stage.

Revenue Source, Demand Risk, and Finance

SPV revenues depend on the project's availability, the level of user fees, demand volume, and the term of the contract. The relevance of each factor varies across projects, but revenues can be classified along two dimensions: the source of payments and the extent to which the SPV is made to bear demand risk.

Provided that the SPV meets the minimum quality and availability standards, demand for most PPP projects is largely exogenous. Despite the fact that they cannot affect demand, many PPPs are made to bear demand risk. When revenues are derived primarily from user fees, SPVs assume two types of project risks associated with demand. The first is the risk that the project will fail and never repay the creditors. This risk represents a market test of the quality of the project and is correctly assigned to creditors. The second risk stems from the fact that the term of the concession contract is fixed (say, at 40 years). As discussed in Chapter 3, this means that a profitable project may fail to repay the debt over the contract term – because of adverse initial macroeconomic conditions, for instance. Even when the primary source of revenues is the procuring authority, the contract may tie payments to the demand for the project over a fixed term, with so-called shadow tolls (or fees). In both these cases, bondholders bear the uncertainty that demand over the term of the contract may not generate sufficient revenues to meet debt payments on schedule. As residual claimants, sponsors face even more risk and expect large profits in compensation.

Contracts can be designed to eliminate or reduce the connection between project revenues and demand. This limits the second type of risk and therefore lowers both rents to the sponsor and the return bondholders demand. When the source of revenues is the procuring authority, the contract that eliminates this risk has a fixed term, with payments contingent on the availability of the infrastructure (hence the term *availability payments*). When user fees are the main source of revenue and demand for the project is high, the appropriate contract is the present-value-of-revenue (PVR) contract, which specifies a fixed present value of revenues under a variable length contract (see Chapter 3). In either case, the contract largely eliminates demand risk. Revenue risk is reduced to failing to meet clearly defined performance standards.

All things considered, financiers prefer predictable cash flows (see Fitch Ratings, 2010). Consequently, availability contracts and flexible-term contracts tend to receive higher ratings than contracts in which the concession bears considerable demand risk.

The Role of Credit Rating Agencies and Insurance Providers

While the relationship between bondholders and the SPV is distant, management behavior is still monitored (somewhat loosely) by credit rating agencies and insurance companies while bonds remain outstanding. The financial crisis of 2008 brought to light the various deficiencies of the reliance on rating agencies and monoline bond insurers. The analysis that follows assumes a reformed system of credit rating agencies and credit insurance companies that are not subject to the conflicts of interest that beset the industry up to 2008.

The role of credit rating agencies and credit insurance companies is essential to the issuance of bonds. The credit rating agency issues a so-called shadow rating of the SPV. With this rating, the SPV buys credit insurance that increases the rating of its bond to investment grade or higher (for instance from BBB to AAA), and the bonds are then sold to institutional and other investors. In a correctly functioning market, the insurance premium should be equal to the difference in effective risk premiums between the insured and the shadow rating. In the example, this corresponds to the difference in risk premiums between AAA and BBB bonds. This premium varies over the life of the project, as risk perceptions and circumstances change. The bond covenants mandate that the SPV pay the premiums required to preserve the initial risk rating of the bond. This creates the correct incentives for the SPV, as its costs increase with the perceived riskiness of the bonds.

Credit rating companies worry most about the impact of the various risks facing the project on the SPV's ability to make the scheduled debt payments. This requires the analysis of the expected value and volatility of the project's net cash flow. In addition, credit rating agencies penalize poor information, ambiguities, complexity, and discretion in laws or contracts. The rating of a bond thus depends on the quality and timeliness of the information revealed by the SPV; the opinions of experts (favorable reports by independent experts generally increase ratings); the quality of laws and institutions that have a bearing on the project; and the clarity and potential for conflicts in the web of contracts. In terms of contract theory, credit rating companies punish contract incompleteness.

In addition to the risks inherently related to the economics of the project – that is, construction, operating, and revenue risks – the evaluations also take into account exchange rate, political, and country risks.

Nowadays, when the credit insurance companies are unavailable and there is little confidence in credit rating agencies, many institutional investors do their own bond evaluations and invest with no insurance. In the United States, banks provide letters of credit for bonds (Yescombe, private communication).

Project Finance versus Corporate Finance
A PPP infrastructure project can be set up either as a project within a company, using corporate debt for financing, or as a stand-alone project incorporated as a special purpose vehicle, or SPV. While the second form has larger transactions costs, it provides advantages that compensate for the added cost of the complex structure of the SPV. Most PPP contracts use project finance because it is useful in raising long-term financing for major projects.

A characteristic of project finance is that sponsors provide no guarantees beyond the right to be paid from the project's cash flows. Nevertheless, sponsors need to attract large amounts of resources to reduce the financing cost, as owning equity is expensive. This leaves them highly leveraged, typically with lenders providing 70 percent to 100 percent of their funds. The level of leverage depends on the volatility of revenues – and when these are very volatile, the project may not be bankable. Governments sometimes provide revenue insurance to improve the bankability of a project. Better alternatives, such as PVR and availability contracts, also allow for high levels of gearing. Conversely, technically complex projects require higher levels of sponsor equity.

There are various reasons for the choice of SPVs and project finance over corporate finance in PPPs. Because SPVs use high levels of leverage, the expected return on equity increases, even after adjusting for the higher financing costs. Moreover, it is more difficult to raise equity than to raise debt, especially on projects with no history, and this leads to higher leverage.

During the construction phase, by separating the project from a larger sponsoring corporation, an SPV precludes underinvestment in the project caused by competition for resources within the sponsor. Moreover, when a PPP is established as a division within a corporation, the large cash flows the project produces during the operational phase are subject to costly agency problems. Otherwise the corporation may divert the revenues from their primary role of repaying the debt contracted to fund the project. An infrastructure SPV does not have growth opportunities, so the possibility of diverting resources away from creditors is very limited, in contrast to the case of a division within a large corporation. Hence, the project's cash flow can be credibly pledged to pay bondholders, and this allows for high leverage.

A final reason for isolating the project within an SPV is that it reduces the possibility of contaminating the healthy corporation with the problems of the independent entity. Even when a subsidiary's problems do not threaten the parent corporation's financial stability, financial distress in the subsidiary affects the credit conditions facing the corporation.

These financial advantages of SPVs would be offset if stand-alone projects forego important scope economies. As argued earlier, however, few productive efficiency gains can be realized by pooling multiple large PPP projects whose demand is normally location based. Any gains that can be realized by sponsoring several PPP projects – such as previous experience and lobbying proficiency – can be achieved by sponsoring several SPVs. Tirole suggests that linking the fates of two independent projects allows higher levels of leverage than when the projects remain independent, but we believe this effect is comparatively less important in this instance (2006, Chapter 4).

5.2 The PPP Premium

A recurrent criticism of PPPs is that they cost more per dollar of financing than public debt – the so-called PPP premium. For example, the trade magazine *Euromoney* gives the following argument for public financing: "The other solution (to highway finance) is to finance the project wholly in the public sector, either with government or multilateral funds. It is, after all, more expensive to raise debt on a project finance basis. When considered alongside the guarantees and commitments which have to be provided to attract commercial finance, the best approach would be to borrow on a sovereign basis."[6]

The numbers quoted for this cost difference vary widely. According to Yescombe, the cost of capital for a PPP used to be 200–300 basis points higher than the cost of public funds (2007, p. 18). This difference has doubled since the credit crisis. He also shows that the spread over the lender's cost of funds lies in the range of 75–150 basis points, with highway projects being on the upper limit (Yescombe, 2007, p. 150). Hence, when governments decide

---

[6]　Cited in Klein (1997, p. 29).

between public provision and PPPs, they trade off a lower cost of funds under public provision against the supposedly higher efficiency of a PPP.

Other authors, however, argue that there is no PPP premium. One line of argument claims that general government default risk subsumes bondholder risk under public provision. Moreover, public debt is cheaper because the public implicitly absorbs the risk through potentially higher taxes or lower public expenditures in case of imminent default on all government debt. As John Kay (1993) noted, "The view that 'private sector capital costs more' is naïve because the cost of debt both to governments and to private firms is influenced predominantly by the perceived risk of default rather than an assessment of the quality of returns from the specific investment. We would lend to government even if we thought it would burn the money or fire it off into space, and we do lend it for both these purposes."[7] In other words, while many failed projects go unaccounted for under public provision because taxpayers assume the costs of this risk, under a PPP these risks are made explicit and priced, increasing the measured financing cost of a PPP project. This merely reflects a just reward for carrying those risks.

Diversification and Contracting

Regarding other risks, financial economists distinguish between systematic risk – which varies systematically with the market or the economy – and project-specific risk. The project's systematic risk cannot be diversified and should affect public and private financing in the same way.[8] Is there a prima facie reason to think that the public sector can be better at diversifying exogenous risks than PPP financiers?

With perfect capital markets, the diversification that government participation can achieve in a large number of projects is also achievable through the capital market, so no PPP premium would exist in this case. As Hirshleifer pointed out, "The efficient discount rate, assuming perfect markets, is the market rate implicit in the valuation of private assets whose returns are 'comparable' to the public investment in question – where 'comparable' means having the same proportionate time-state distribution of returns" (1966, p. 272). Hence, the PPP premium and the alleged financial advantage of public provision would seem to rest on capital market

---

[7] Ibid.

[8] As Shugart (2010) argued, if part of the systematic risk premium would be something peculiar to the equity markets, then part of the PPP premium would be a true additional cost for PPPs that would not apply to projects financed by the public sector (taxpayers). But we see little reason to think that this is the case.

imperfections that give an edge to diversification opportunities available to the government. Interestingly, this does not require that project returns be independent of the economy (the assumption of the Arrow-Lind theorem), but only that some options of risk spreading available to the government are unavailable through the capital market (see Brainard and Dolbear, 1971).

In the real world, there are transaction costs that preclude the existence of complete markets and limit diversification through the capital market. However, diversification opportunities available to the government must be weighed against the administrative cost of its bureaucracy. But even if the government had an advantage in risk bearing, we show next that PPP contracts exist that assign all exogenous risk to the government.

To see this, consider the following scenario: demand for the infrastructure is uncertain, so that the consumer surplus at time t, CS_t, and user fee revenues, R_t, are random variables determined by the state of demand, v, that is, by one possible trajectory of demand realizations. The upfront investment, I, is the same in all demand states and operating and maintenance costs are zero. Finally, the PPP firm is selected in a competitive auction that dissipates rents.

The upper half of Table 5.1 depicts the distribution of the present value of cash flows and surpluses in one demand state, v, for alternative sources of funds and procurement mechanisms. Rows distinguish between the revenue sources (user fees versus taxes). Columns distinguish between governance structures (public provision versus PPPs). Within PPPs, alternative contractual forms are possible, depending on the source of revenues.

Under public provision, PVR and availability payments are identical (columns 1 and 2 in the table). This is our main claim: independent of the source of funds, PPP contracts exist that replicate in all demand states the surplus and cash flow distribution of public provision and have the same impact on the intertemporal public budget.

To see this, consider first the case in which financing comes from user fees. Under public provision, the project is built at cost I, and the firm receives I before the infrastructure becomes operational (we assume competitive tendering that dissipates all rents). Hence, taxpayers pay I upfront, collect $R_0^\infty(v)$ in state v, and receive $R_0^\infty(v) - I$ in present value, where X_a^b denotes the present value of X_t between $t = a$ and $t = b$, as of time $t = 0$. Users, however, receive a net surplus equal to $CS_0^\infty(v) - R_0^\infty(v)$. Under a PVR contract, taxpayers save I up front, but they relinquish user fee revenue during the length of the concession, which is equal to I in present value (given that the competitive assumption means that the winning bid will ask for I in present value of revenues). Because the state collects user fees after $CS_0^\infty(v) - R_0^\infty(v)$, as with public provision. This confirms that any risk

Table 5.1. *Risk allocation, source of revenues, and contractual form*

Sources of revenue	Contractual form		
		PPP	
	Public provision (1)	PVR contract (2)	Fixed-term contract (3)
User fee finance			
Users	$CS_0^\infty(v) - R_0^\infty(v)$	$CS_0^\infty(v) - R_0^\infty(v)$	$CS_0^\infty(v) - R_0^\infty(v)$
Taxpayers	$R_0^\infty(v) - I$	$R_0^\infty(v) - I$	$R_0^\infty(v) - R_0^T(v)$
Firms	$I - I$	$I - I$	$R_0^T(v) - I$
		Availability payment	*Fixed-term shadow toll*
Tax finance			
Users	$CS_0^\infty(v)$	$CS_0^\infty(v)$	$CS_0^\infty(v)$
Taxpayers	$-I$	$-I$	$-R_0^T(v)$
Firms	$I - I$	$I - I$	$R_0^T(v) - I$

Notation. v = state of demand; CS = consumer surplus; R = user fee or shadow toll revenue; I = upfront investment; X_s^t = present discounted value of X between times s and t, as of time 0; T = length of fixed-term contract.

Assumptions. The table depicts cash flows and social surplus in a given demand state v (corresponding to present discounted value of user-fee revenue in the state) for alternative sources of funds and contractual arrangements. Rows distinguish between sources of funds (user fees and taxes); columns between procurement forms (public provision and PPPs). Demand for the infrastructure is uncertain, so consumer surplus, CS, and user-fee revenues, R, are random variables of the demand state, v. The upfront investment, I, is the same in all demand states, and operating and maintenance costs are zero. Firms are selected in competitive auctions that dissipate all rents.

diversification advantage for the government can be realized with a PPP contract of the PVR type.

Now consider a fixed-term PPP that lasts T years (column 3). The concessionaire collects $R_0^T(v)$ with a surplus of $R_0^T(v) - I$, a random variable; in contrast, she faces no risk under a PVR contract. Taxpayers receive $R_T^\infty(v)$, and, in general, their risk falls.[9] A fixed-term contract thus shifts risk from taxpayers to the concessionaire because there is uncertainty about demand for the project during the fixed term T.

Next consider projects that are fully financed by taxpayers. Again, with public provision the project is built at cost I, which the firm receives before

---

[9] For any process with independent increments, as well as any stationary nondeterministic process, it is easy to show that the standard deviation of R_T^∞ as of time zero is decreasing in T. It follows that with public provision or a PVR contract, the standard deviation of taxpayers' discounted revenue will be higher than under a fixed-term PPP.

the infrastructure becomes operational – taxpayers pay I upfront. When a PPP is financed with availability payments, the timing of disbursements differs, but the present value of payments is the same – I. Hence, neither the taxpayers nor the concessionaire bear risk, and the impact of the project on the intertemporal public budget is the same in both cases. Thus, part of the observed PPP premium may reflect faulty contract design rather than a fundamental disadvantage of PPPs. Box 5.2 further illustrates this point with a concrete example.

Box 5.2 *Faulty contract design and the PPP premium*

To see the effect of contracting on the PPP premium, we consider a brief example, summarized in Figure 5.4. Assume a project that requires an upfront investment of $I = 100$. Annual user fee revenue is assumed constant over time, equal to 7.9 and 12.8 in the low- and high-demand states, which are equally likely. Finally, we assume that firms cannot fully diversify risk (for example, to provide incentives to owners or managers) and have a concave utility function.

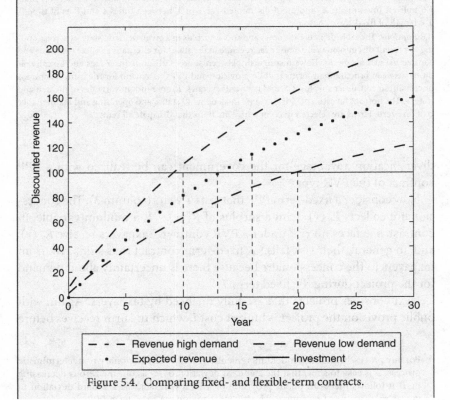

Figure 5.4. Comparing fixed- and flexible-term contracts.

In the figure, the dashed line shows discounted revenue in the low-demand state and the dashed-dotted line shows discounted revenue in the high-demand state. The dotted line is the expected discounted revenue.

The PVR contract lasts until the firm collects 100, that is, 10 years if demand is high and 20 years if demand is low. The firm bears no risk and therefore charges no risk premium. The implicit interest therefore equals the risk-free discount rate of 5 percent, and there is no PPP premium.

Consider next a fixed-term contract and assume that firms bid on the shortest contract term. If firms are risk neutral, the winner will bid a contract length that ensures expected discounted revenue of 100 on average. The contract length in this case: 13.2 years. If the firm cannot fully diversify risk, it will demand a risk premium. In our example, the contract length in this case is 16 years.[10] The firm's expected revenue is larger than 100: in our example, the expected revenue at 16 years is 114. Hence, there is a PPP premium with a fixed-term contract and risk averse firms: the firm invests 100 and expects discounted revenue of 114.

It follows that a PVR contract can attract investors at lower interest rates than the usual fixed-term PPP contract. The realized sample path of user-fee revenues are the same under both contractual forms, but the franchise term is demand contingent only under a PVR contract. If demand is low, the franchise holder of a fixed-term contract may default; in contrast, a PVR concession is extended until toll revenue equals the bid, which rules out default. The downside under PVR is that bondholders do not know when they will be repaid, but this risk carries a lower cost than default risk. ∎

PPPs financed via taxes have sometimes resorted to shadow fees. That is, the state pays a fee to the concessionaire for every user of the infrastructure for a fixed number of years, T. This type of PPP contract not only shifts risk to the concessionaire, but also creates risk. Because the concessionaire now bears risk, a PPP premium should be observed (lower right corner of Table 5.1). Viewed from this perspective, a shadow fee contract consists in adding a lottery to an availability contract. The firm and taxpayers are forced to participate in a zero-sum lottery in which whatever one party wins is lost by the other. This leads to a risk premium that is not inherent to PPPs, but results from a specific contractual form.[11]

Risk and Efficiency of PPPs
There are various reasons society may be better off under a PPP than under public provision, and these generally impose additional risk on the private

---

[10] With the approximation for the risk premium in proposition 9 in Engel, Fischer, and Galetovic (2001), this corresponds to a utility function with coefficient of relative risk aversion equal to 2.15.

[11] Of course, a lottery is by definition nonsystematic risk and should be fully diversifiable through perfect capital markets. Nevertheless, it doesn't make much sense to add risk to a contract considering that in the real world there are transaction costs.

party. First, firms control the infrastructure assets during the life of the contract under a PPP, so innovations that use the assets more efficiently do not require extensive negotiations with the regulator. Under public provision, introducing innovations is very cumbersome. For example, investing in cost-reducing and other efficiency-enhancing activities usually implies assuming additional risk, which is likely to increase the cost of capital for the firm. The flip side is that if the innovation succeeds, life-cycle costs will be lower than under public provision. This suggests that there will be more innovations under PPPs than under public provision.

A second argument in favor of PPPs, as discussed earlier in this chapter, is that project finance is structured so as to provide incentives to internalize life-cycle cost considerations during the construction phase. These incentives are not present under public provision.

More generally, one of the main points of a PPP is to shift endogenous risk to the concessionaire to prevent moral hazard and to strengthen incentives to cut costs and provide adequate service quality. Unless the concessionaire is risk neutral, he will charge for bearing that risk. Moreover, these risks are not diversifiable in the capital market for if they could be diversified, there would be no incentive to improve performance in the first place. The "right" PPP premium would compare financing costs under public provision, coupled to an incentive contract where the agent bears endogenous risk, with the financing costs under a PPP. In practice, however, the inability to make remunerations depend on performance means that traditional provision cannot transfer endogenous risks to agents.

Transaction Costs

The complexity of the relationship between the sponsor, who owns the SPV, and the procurement agency, which oversees the contract and certifies compliance, creates transaction costs. These could potentially be so high that they negate the other advantages of PPPs. Thus it is sometimes argued that PPPs are financially more expensive because they require legal, technical, and financial advisors, as well as specialists in demand risk estimation. These costs can reach 10 percent of total project costs (Dos Santos Senna and Dutra Michel, 2008; Yescombe, 2007, p. 26). These costs do not scale with the size of the project, so for small projects a PPP is impracticable unless several projects can be packaged as copies of a single project (Yescombe, 2007). These administrative expenses, which duplicate the studies of the procuring authority, are not necessarily wasted, as they provide a check on the excessively optimistic numbers provided by both the government and the project sponsor. When this

Table 5.2. *PFI lead times by sector*

Sector	Procurement dates	Financial closure (months)	Upper and lower bounds
Health	12/94–12/98	40	22–60
Schools	03/97–12/99	23	15–25
Defense	11/94–09/99	23	18–32
Custodial facilities and prisons	03/97–11/99	21.4	14–25
Roads	03/86–11/95	18	15–20
Trams and light rail	03/86–11/95	22.3	13–30

Source: H. M. Treasury (2003).

factor is considered, the additional expense might be partly justified if it reduces the life-cycle costs of the project.

The relationship between the sponsor and the procurement agency, which is absent under public provision, also introduces the potential for conflicts that may affect the flow of revenues to the concessionaire and debt holders. These contractual risks include the reasonableness of performance tests, the penalty mechanisms in the concession contract, the experience of the sponsor and operator in the industry or country, the transparency of the tender agreements, the strength of legal precedent, the strength of the conflict resolution framework, and the political support for PPPs. Consequently, this is a factor that leads to a higher risk premium under PPPs. PPPs, however, make apparent risks that the public assumes under public provision, so again the higher risk premium is not necessarily an artifact of PPPs.

Finally, another source of added costs is the long lead time PPPs require, which is usually longer than the lead time for public provision. The complexities inherent to the SPV form, plus the many eventualities that must be considered in a long-term contractual relationship, explain the longer preparation periods. This can be seen in Table 5.2, which shows the time to financial closure (before beginning to build) in the United Kingdom. Because financiers usually recover these costs through the rate they charge, this tends to increase the PPP premium. Note, however, that in some countries with weak public management systems, PPPs may have an advantage given the inefficiencies of traditional provision.

Against this longer lead time, in the United Kingdom a project is slightly more likely to be completed on time and on budget under a PPP than under public provision (Table 5.3). As discussed in Chapter 2, a more

Table 5.3. *Percentage of projects that were on time and on budget*

Percent				
Project status	H-M Treasury report		NAO report	
	PFI	Non-PFI	PFI	Non-PFI
On time	88	30	69	65
On budget	79	28	65	54

Sources: H. M. Treasury (2003); NAO (2009).

careful NAO study finds a smaller advantage for PFI and it is not altogether clear that the additional lead times translate into higher life-cycle costs of the project.

Case evidence from other countries suggests that shorter time frames for construction are common for transportation projects. According to the U.S. National Conference of State Legislatures: "PPPs often can result in significant project cost and time savings compared to traditional procurement. Causes can include direct incentives to the private contractor for on-time delivery; use of warranties ... or performance-based contracting; competition among bidders; transfer of risk to the private sector for cost and schedule overruns or revenue shortfalls; and lifecycle efficiencies" (Rall, Reed, and Farber, 2010, p. 9).

5.3 Conclusion

The alleged financial advantages of PPPs are one of the main reasons for their popularity. Newspaper articles often claim that PPPs release government funds and expand the set of projects that governments can undertake. As we discuss in the next chapter, however, there is no fiscal reason to prefer PPPs over public provision. Hence, the case for PPPs must rest on efficiency gains rather than on their purported fiscal advantages.

Although the rates required by the private party of a PPP are higher than those facing the government, PPP financing is not inherently more costly than public provision financed with public debt. With adequate contracting, PPPs can replicate the intertemporal risk profile of public provision. This suggests that the so-called PPP premium arises as a result of the implicit guarantee provided by taxpayers for government debt; faulty contract design that inefficiently assigns exogenous risks to the private partner; and cost-cutting incentives embedded in PPPs. Consequently, the observed higher cost of capital under PPP should not be interpreted as evidence against this contractual option.

PPPs require sophisticated financial engineering. Unlike public provision, in its standard configuration, a PPP isolates the infrastructure and its cash flows by creating a special purpose vehicle, or SPV. This organizational form conforms well with the basic economics of infrastructure projects and contributes to better accountability.

Bibliographic Notes

Yescombe (2002) provides a comprehensive introduction to project finance; his 2007 book is a clear and complete description of PPP finance. See also the recent book by Weber and Alfen (2010). Whether infrastructure is an asset class by itself is discussed by Inderst (2010). Bitsch, Buchner, and Kaserer (2010) examine the financial performance of infrastructure funds. Stewart-Smith (1995) discusses private financing of infrastructure in emerging markets. Theoretical analyses of PPP finance include de Bettignies and Ross (2009) and Trujillo and colleagues (1998). Jean Tirole's (2006) discussion on financing stand-alone projects in his corporate finance textbook is very useful. Our analysis of SPVs is based on the modern theory of the scope of firms – see Williamson (1976, 1985).

The classic reference arguing that public financing is cheaper is Arrow and Lind (1970). Brainard and Dolbear (1971) put the Arrow-Lind theorem into perspective; for a recent and insightful criticism, see Baumstark and Gollier (2013). For more on the controversy, see Brealey, Cooper, and Habib (1997). Klein (1997) argued that the PPP premium probably just reflects that governments can tax to pay off their debts. The same point is stressed by Jenkinson (2003), who argues that in public projects taxpayers and users provide the equivalent of equity finance, as they bear residual losses. A complete discussion is in Shugart (2010). The comparison of fixed- and flexible-term contracts (Box 5.2) is based on Engel, Fischer, and Galetovic (1997b). The relation between risk and incentives is studied theoretically by Iossa and Martimort (2012) and Engel, Fischer, and Galetovic (2012).

Public Finance

During the 1980s and 1990s, many governments, under the argument of the increased efficiency of firms under private management, privatized utilities and spent the proceeds. Similarly, many governments chose to use PPPs for new infrastructure for two reasons: first, they believed that PPPs relaxed constraints on government budgets; second, under fiscal accounting rules that applied at the time, this organizational form allowed them to circumvent budgetary controls on public investment. In this chapter we show that the first belief is incorrect and PPPs do not relax the fiscal budget constraint. Moreover, we present evidence showing that governments used PPPs to evade budgetary controls on spending. We also provide specific fiscal accounting proposals to eliminate this possibility.

6.1 Fiscal Accounting

One of the drivers of PPPs is that governments want to indulge in public works even when restricted by budgetary constraints (see Box 6.1 for examples). For this reason, organizations that set accounting standards have struggled to determine when a PPP project should be included on the balance sheet of the public sector.

Box 6.1 *PPPs of existing facilities and government spending*

Greenfield and brownfield PPP projects typically involve upfront investments either in new infrastructure or in a major revamp of an existing facility. Sometimes, however, an existing facility that requires little or no new investment is franchised and a PPP is set up, as with the Chicago Skyway (see Chapter 2.3). In such a PPP the private party maintains and operates the facility and collects user fees in exchange for a

---

large upfront payment to the government.[1] This kind of PPP is attractive for governments that want to reassign long-term assets to more productive purposes, especially if they believe that a private party will extract more value from the infrastructure. Nevertheless, often the main reason behind such PPPs is the government's desire to spend the upfront payment, which is bad fiscal policy. ∎

As far as the risk profile of the government budget is concerned, PPPs are much closer to public provision than to privatization (see Section 6.2). Our starting point to derive this insight is that when thinking about the risk allocation PPPs imply, what matters is the volatility of the discounted budget and not the fluctuations in annual revenues.

This has interesting implications: for a PVR contract of a high-demand project, the PPP replicates the net cash flow streams of public provision, state by state (see Table 5.1 in the previous chapter).[2] All residual risk is transferred to the government and users, and the concessionaire recovers the upfront investment, I, in all states, as in the case of public provision. By contrast, under privatization, the project is sold for a one-time payment, and all risk is transferred to the firm. Moreover, the link between the project and the public budget is permanently severed. This is not the case with a PPP, where cash flows from the project replace either taxes or subsidies at the margin. The conclusion, then, is that from a public finance perspective there is a strong presumption that PPPs are analogous to public provision – in essence, they remain public projects and should be treated as such in the government balance sheet.

Nevertheless, because PPPs are relatively recent, there is little agreement over how to account for them on the government's balance sheet. As Eurostat (2010) pointed out, the key accounting issue is the classification of the assets involved in the PPP contract. If they are classified as government assets, they immediately influence the deficit and government debt. By contrast, if they are classified as assets of the concessionaire, the impact on the government deficit is spread over the duration of the contract. Hence, if PPP assets are classified as private, governments can keep them off their balance sheets, thereby avoiding spending and debt caps. Under public provision, however, caps on spending or net fiscal debt are in principle more effective

---

[1] When the user fee revenue just covers operations and maintenance, it is an O&M contract, not a PPP.

[2] Recall that a high-demand project is one whose revenues finance capital and operating expenses in all demand scenarios.

in controlling the bias toward spending anticipation, because projects must be included in the budget.

One systematic treatment of PPPs is in Eurostat (2010). If user fees are the main revenue sources of the PPP, as in a toll road, Eurostat considers the assets private during the life of the contract.[3] By contrast, if most of the concessionaire's revenues are government payments (as in an availability contract or with shadow tolls), the classification of assets depends on who bears construction, availability, and demand risks.

Thus if the private partner bears construction risk and either availability or demand risk, Eurostat recommends that assets built by PPPs be classified as nongovernmental and thus recorded off the balance sheet. For this reason, a basic concept in classifying PPPs as off balance sheet is risk transfer to the private sector, because this implies that the private sponsor "has skin in the game" and that the project does not entail a present or future cost to the government. However, these general principles allow for considerable discretion. Governments can game Eurostat's rules because of its formal nature. For example, it has problems in the case of minimum revenue guarantees. Contingent guarantees are assumed to transfer risk if they are not likely to be called, and this ambiguity allows for excessive discretion.

The United Kingdom's generally accepted accounting principles (GAAP) are less formal and focus more on the substance of risk transfer. These rules consider a project on the balance sheet under any of the following conditions: if the public works authority (PWA) is responsible for the debt under default; if the level of risk is excessive and would only be assumed if lenders face no risks; or if the PWA decides ex post the conditions by which the PFI contract is fulfilled.[4] Moreover, the U.K. GAAP requires that any other risks borne by the PWA be quantified and their NPV be compared to the NPV of the project. If the remaining risks represent a substantial fraction of the NPV of the project, the project should be on the government's balance sheet. This means that the "U.K. GAAP only included the liabilities if the balance of risk and reward was with the public sector" (House of Lords Select Committee on Economic Affairs, 2010, Chapter 3). However,

---

[3] It should be pointed out that Eurostat calls this a *concession*; in the manual, the term *PPP* is only used for contracts such that the majority of the partner's revenue comes from government payments. Thus a toll road PPP would be called a toll road *concession*, while the term *PPP* would be reserved for a road franchised under availability payments or shadow tolls. By contrast, we make no distinction between PPPs and concessions in this book. Our definition of either one of these concepts includes all possible combinations of revenue sources (user fees and government transfers) as compensation for the firm's upfront investment.

[4] See Yescombe (2007, p. 72).

as mentioned in Section 2.1, because the interpretation of "balance" was left to public bodies and their auditors, this led to most PFI projects not being included in the public sector net debt statistics. This changed in 2009, when the U.K. accounting practices began to abide by the IFRS standards. Under this standard, assets that are controlled by the public sector, including most PFI projects, have to be included in the departmental balance sheets (House of Lords Select Committee on Economic Affairs, 2010). Nonetheless, as mentioned in Section 2.1, in practice there exist two parallel accounting standards (the more demanding IFRIC 12 and the older GAAP) and PFI investments remain excluded from national debt calculations.

How should PPPs be accounted for in the budget? The key point is that PPPs change the timing of government revenues and disbursements and the composition of financing, but do not alter the present value of the discounted budget. They should therefore be treated just as standard government investments. To see why, consider a PPP project built in one year, with neither operational nor maintenance costs, which is fully financed by future payments from the budget; and also consider a similar project built under public provision. In the first case, under current fiscal accounting there is neither deficit nor debt. However, each year until the end of the contract, the government has to pay a predetermined amount to remunerate the capital cost of the concessionaire. At the end of the contract, the government becomes the owner of the asset. In the second case, the government initially increases its debt by the amount of the loan necessary to build the project, incurs a budget deficit that same year, under current fiscal rules, and obtains an asset to balance the increased debt. Each year thereafter it pays down the debt and when the debt is run down (assuming the same payments as in the previous case), it has the asset and no debt nor payments. From a correct accounting point of view, a PPP just substitutes debt with the concessionaire for standard public debt. Thus, there is no reason to treat those PPPs differently from projects under public provision. It follows that on the award of such a PPP, the present value of the contract should be counted as a public capital expenditure and public debt should be increased by the same amount. Over the life of the concession debt must be run down in the books.

Our proposal runs somewhat contrary to the Eurostat rules, and it is interesting to discuss why. Even under public provision, construction risks are usually allocated to the private firm. Hence, Eurostat rules imply that the government can take the PPP off the balance sheet when the concessionaire assumes either availability or demand risk. The problem with Eurostat is that it takes a static view of risk allocation. Once we use an intertemporal approach, it is clear that, even if the firm bears all the demand risk during the life of the contract, the discounted budget still is the residual risk claimant. Furthermore, when quality is contractible, as arguably is the case for most PPP investments in the transportation sector, demand risk will be mainly exogenous and therefore does not provide useful incentives. To the extent that taxpayers bear exogenous risk at a lower cost than the firm, the optimal contract then eliminates risk for the firm. Thus, the effect on the government budget is identical to that of public provision.

Note that the adoption of our proposal would require changes in the way that government statistics are recorded.[5] The reason is as follows. The basic building block of accounting and macroeconomic statistics is the institutional unit – the basic unit that generates statistics or accounting data from its economic activities. In the case of PPPs, the institutional location of the SPV largely determines the accounting convention followed by governments; only if the SPV is controlled by the government, transactions related to PPPs are automatically consolidated within the government accounts. Therefore, many countries push PPPs off the balance sheet by classifying SPVs as private sector entities. Even when the SPV follows adequate international standards (normally requested by stakeholders for surveillance purposes), their transactions have no impact on government accounts. By contrast, our proposal argues that infrastructure procured via a PPP should be considered public. In our view, it should be indifferent whether the entity performing the function is part of the public sector or privately owned.

Some might argue that counting privately financed investment as public debt may worsen the bias against public spending in infrastructure, which is the result of political incentives, perhaps excessively stringent limits on fiscal borrowing and faulty accounting rules that treat investment as current expenditure (see Blanchard and Giavazzi, 2004). According to this argument, keeping PPPs off the balance sheet is a second best remedy that mitigates the bias and increases the output of socially worthwhile infrastructure projects, which might get funding because they are kept off the balance sheet.

The easy answer to this criticism is that the bias against infrastructure spending should be addressed, changing the incentives within the public sector and improving public accounting. The more realistic answer is that the remedy hypothesis assumes a virtuous government. Nevertheless, spending limits exist precisely because governments want to overspend. It is doubtful in principle and, given the experience with PPPs so far, probably wrong in practice to believe that governments will use off-balance-sheet vehicles wisely and with prudence.

---

[5]   We thank Katja Funke, Isabel Rial, and Shamsuddin Tareq for pointing this out to us.

Government Revenue Guarantees

As mentioned earlier, some concessions can be financed in part or completely with user fees, and governments commonly grant revenue guarantees to concessionaires, especially when concessions last a fixed term. Guarantees are contingent subsidies. As such, they have effect on the discounted budget, but their contingent nature makes it difficult to account for them in the budget.

Under current accounting standards, future obligations will probably remain hidden (Hemming, 2006, p. 40). Cash accounting makes guarantees apparent only when they are paid, in which case they appear as current expenditure. Accrual accounting, in turn, records the guarantee as a government liability only if the government considers that the probability of making a payment is higher than 50 percent and can make a reasonable estimate of the payment. Even then, unless the government makes a provision and sets aside the funds, guarantees are only recorded when they are called. Worse, most countries have poor records of guarantees, and, when information exists, it is locked in individual agencies and ministries (Hemming, 2006, p. 42). Some countries, such as Chile, Colombia, and New Zealand, have attempted to quantify guarantees within an accrual framework by estimating the expected outlays and correcting for the degree of risk involved (for example, via value-at-risk-type measures). Nevertheless, any rule that relies on a probabilistic assessment can be easily manipulated, as probabilities are ultimately a matter of judgment. Guarantees thus soften the budget constraint of the incumbent government, allowing it to sidestep normal budgetary procedures and congressional oversight.

With our proposal, government guarantees do not warrant special treatment because they are subsumed in the obligations of the government. When the full amount invested is accounted as a public capital expenditure, with a corresponding increase in public debt, guarantees are implicitly included, and there is no need to make value judgments on the cost of a contingent guarantee.

Accounting for capital and debt payments is somewhat trickier. As in the case of the optimal contract, this "debt" is backed by a combination of user-fee revenue, guarantees, and possible renegotiations of the concession contract. These different items are combined in different proportions as events unfold. In the case of fixed-term PPPs, the private partner assumes the demand risk and may receive capital gains or losses over the life of the concession. This requires a convention for the treatment of project revenues and the gradual extinction of the guarantee as the concession unfolds. In any case, under our proposal the full cost of the project is recognized as debt, so it follows that it will be extinguished when the concession ends.

Box 6.2 *The Ryrie Rules*

While there seems to be considerable confusion about how to account for PPPs in the government's budget and on the balance sheet, it is worth mentioning that the problems they might cause seem to have been understood during the 1980s in the United Kingdom, well before the introduction of the Private Finance Initiative in 1992. As Heald and McLeod (2002) explain, during the 1980s, the provision of private finance for public projects was governed by the 1981 Ryrie Rules. Under these rules government guarantees were not allowed and private financing could not be additional to public finance – whenever a privately financed project was undertaken, public spending would be reduced, pound for pound. As Heald and McLeod (2002) point out: "The rationale for this provision was that there is little macroeconomic difference between the government borrowing on the market to finance public expenditure generally and the private sector borrowing for essentially public projects. The objective of the Ryrie Rules was to stop ministers from insulating private finance from risk so that it could be used to circumvent public expenditure constraints." It can be easily seen that whenever there is a spending cap, this provision is equivalent to our proposal to count PPP projects as current investment.

It is telling that the Ryrie Rules were formally abandoned in 1989 and that from then on the British Treasury promoted private financing as additional to public investment. This suggests that incentives and interests rather than ignorance are the reason for the lack of progress in improving PPP accounting rules. ∎

6.2 Relieving Government Budgets

Perhaps the most widespread argument for PPPs among practitioners and politicians is that they relieve strained government budgets. This frees up government resources that can then be spent on other projects with high social return. While this argument seems unobjectionable on its surface, we argued in Section 1.4 that this reasoning is wrong.

An alternative argument for PPPs, which is also related to public finance, is that of the lower cost of public funds. According to this doctrine, the government collects distortionary taxes to finance infrastructure projects, whereas the private sector can finance projects without these distortions. It follows that PPPs (or privatization) are to be preferred to public provision. This argument is also incorrect. To see the intuition, denote by f the cost of distortionary taxation, so that a dollar collected by the government has a cost that is more than a dollar to society, say $1 + f$, with $f > 0$. The project can be financed through either user fees or subsidies. The difference between the two financing options is that only subsidies involve distortionary taxation.

The government will save f dollars per dollar invested by the firm in the infrastructure project. However, these savings are offset by the lower revenues government collects: under a PPP, it collects user fees only after the concession ends, while under public provision, it can start collecting user fees once the project is available to users. Thus, for every dollar of user fees given up to the concessionaire, the government forgoes the opportunity of reducing distortionary taxation elsewhere in the economy.

Table 5.1 (see Chapter 5) can be used to compare the two effects. In demand state v, discounted government revenues are the same under both public provision and a PVR contract: $R_0^\infty(v) - I$. As long as the cost-of-public-funds parameter, f, does not vary over time, we conclude that the government collects the same amount under both contractual forms. This allows it to reduce taxes elsewhere in the economy by a discounted value $f[R_0^\infty(v) - I]$ in excess of what it collects from the facility. Thus, user fee and subsidy financing are perfect substitutes at the margin, and the distortionary cost of taxation does not provide a rationale for the use of PPPs.

Resource-Constrained Governments

Many financially constrained governments see PPPs as an answer to providing infrastructure services. According to this view, PPPs allow credit-rationed governments to invest in additional socially profitable projects. That is, the current value of the cost of public funds parameter f is much higher – infinite if the government has no access whatsoever to credit – than its expected value in the near future.

To evaluate this claim, we need to classify PPPs into two broad categories: projects whose capital costs can be partially or totally covered by user fees and projects whose capital costs are funded mainly or entirely by future government payments. Examples of the latter are availability contracts, which specify a schedule of capital charges payable in the future and which bind the discounted budget. If firms are prepared to invest in these PPP projects, they are in practice lending funds to the government, which means it is not resource constrained.

However, even PPPs in the first category do not relax the financial restrictions facing the government. If the government can set aside the flow of revenues generated by the project, then it can use these revenues either to pay off the debt under public provision or to pay off the concessionaire under a PPP.[6] And if it cannot credibly protect the flow of revenues from

---

[6] For this mechanism to work, the legal system should be sufficiently sophisticated to ensure that the revenue flows from the PPP can be assigned by (and even mortgaged by) the concessionaire's financial providers, independently of the firm's financial condition. This

creditors or other uses, then neither option is available.[7] Even though PPPs do not help cash-constrained governments, as discussed in Box 6.3, multilaterals may help it set up PPP contracts.

We conclude that, quite generally, PPPs do not free up government resources per se, even though they may do so indirectly if they lead to efficiency gains, a topic we consider in Chapter 5. In many cases, one of the main advantages of PPPs from the government's perspective, if not from the social welfare point of view, is that they allow for investment while keeping future obligations off the balance sheet and outside of parliamentary control. We argue in Box 6.3, however, that there is a role for multilaterals in the case of poor cash-constrained countries, in which case there might be some scope for PPPs as a means of relieving the cash constraint.

Box 6.3 *A role for multilateral organizations*

Consider a poor cash-constrained country that desires to build a revenue-generating infrastructure project. If it tries to obtain a loan to build the project, using the argument that it can repay the loan with the revenues generated by the project, commercial lenders will refuse, because the revenues of a cash-generating project can be appropriated to other purposes rather than repaying the loan. As it is almost impossible to provide guarantees preventing this possibility, a PPP organized as a special purpose vehicle (SPV) is the appropriate mechanism for protecting the private investors in the project (see Chapter 5). However, the cash flow derived from the sunk investment of profitable projects is an attractive target for expropriation by credit-constrained governments.

Partial funding from multilateral banks can reduce this possibility. Multilateral banks protect a project from being expropriated through the clauses associated with their lending. The loans and equity participation of multilateral banks are privileged, for several reasons (Buiter and Fries, 2002). First, any future lending by the multilateral to the borrowing country is conditional on the terms of current loans being in compliance (though there are exceptions to this policy; see Buiter and Fries, 2002). Second, multilaterals have a priority claim over the international reserves of the country, and these claims are senior to those of bilateral and commercial creditors in case of financial distress. Third, the multilateral banks are active in protecting their

---

means that even if the concessionaire is unable to complete the project or goes bankrupt afterward, the revenue flows cannot be captured in the mass of the concessionaire's debt (at least in countries with inefficient bankruptcy systems), but remain available to financiers if the project provides the services it was contracted to perform. In the case of unfinished projects, the financiers might be required to find another construction firm to complete the project before receiving revenue from the project.

[7] Of course, if a law prevents a regional or local government from issuing debt, so that it must pay upfront for any publicly provided infrastructure project, then building a project as a PPP will free up resources.

equity investments in national and international courts of law, and their reputation for this policy increases the cost of noncompliance. This explains the value of the participation of the private investment arm of the multilateral banks in PPP projects in developing countries. By their normally careful lending procedures, multilateral banks can also promote funding by providing information about the quality of the projects in which they invest. ∎

6.3 The Optimal Contract

As a general principle, it is better to select a concessionaire through a competitive auction of a well-defined project (or with clear and enforceable service standards) than through direct negotiations. As discussed in Section 1.4, a competitive auction dissipates the rents that are extracted from users, which can be large because projects often have substantial market power. A competitive auction is also more transparent than selecting the concessionaire via bilateral negotiations, avoiding discretionary decisions by public officials.

Next we discuss our proposals for competitive auction mechanisms, offering different alternatives for projects that are financed mainly via user fees and for those in which user fees do not cover the capital cost of the project.

Tax Finance and Social Cost-Benefit Appraisal

When charging user fees that pay for the capital costs of the project is impossible, there are three alternatives to finance the project. First, the government can use public provision. Second, it can pay the private operator shadow fees (that is, a fixed fee for each user of the infrastructure). Finally, it can pay a fixed periodic fee, contingent on the service quality standard being met, under an availability contract.

As discussed in Chapter 5 (see Table 5.1), fixed-term contracts in which the firm is remunerated with shadow fees create demand risk, as the firm and taxpayers are forced to play risks in a zero-sum game that serves no social purpose. This will increase the risk premium included in the winning bid. Because having the firm bear this risk typically brings no countervailing benefit, this approach should be avoided. The purported benefit of shadow fees is that they avoid white elephants because they are dependent on demand. However, if the government is making all the payments on a project, then that project should undergo careful social evaluation in any case, which would similarly filter out white elephants. It follows that availability contracts should be the preferred option when financing mainly out of general funds, at least for projects with contractible quality (see Chapter 4).

Availability contracts have become increasingly popular in many countries, including France, the United Kingdom, and the United States. Under these contracts, the government contracts with a special purpose vehicle to build public infrastructure (see Chapter 5). In exchange for the project services, the government pays the SPV a fee called a *unitary* payment, which covers principal and interest on the debt plus a return to the SPV's shareholders, known as the *sponsors* or the *private party*. The government also pays an amount based on the expected operating cost for the services, which covers the costs of operations, maintenance, and service provision. The government guarantees that the quality of service keeps to the standards specified in the concession contract by making regular payments conditional on the contracted service being available (H. M. Treasury, 2008b).

These contracts are often auctioned to the firm that demands the lowest annual availability payment. The resulting contract then involves no demand risk for the franchise holder.

Availability payments pay for the upfront investment, and the concessionaire makes a normal profit on this investment regardless of demand realizations. This contract is optimal if no user fees can be charged. As mentioned earlier, the ability to filter white elephants is lost, but the government does not need to compensate the firm for bearing demand risk. Availability contracts can also be used to maintain a network of roads or bridges (see Box 6.4).

Box 6.4 *An availability contract to rebuild 800 bridges in Missouri*

In the summer of 2007, Missouri's Department of Transportation selected a single consortium to rebuild or replace 800 bridges in need of repair and manage them for a minimum of 25 years. The rebuilding and maintenance costs are estimated to lie between $400 million and $600 million (U.S. million), with the State of Missouri making annual payments once the works have been completed. The contract provides strong incentives for the consortium via fines that apply if contract specifications are not met. For example, the company must pay $500 per bridge per day for delays beyond the original construction deadline, $2,000 per day of closure, and $2,000 per day per structure that fails to meet quality levels set out in the contract. ∎

As mentioned before, many PPP projects receive public funds, as in the case of those financed by availability payments or those that collect user fees that are not sufficient to pay for all the costs of the project (construction, operations, and maintenance). In these cases, there is clearly no market test that can measure the private or social profitability of the project. It is therefore necessary to test that the project does not waste resources – that is, that it is not a white elephant. Even when a project stands on its own revenue from user fees, there is no real market test of the real profitability of the project if the successful bidder expects to renegotiate in case of bad realizations of the states of nature (see Chapter 1.3). Hence, in all these cases, a realistic social cost-benefit analysis of the project is necessary. This should provide at least a modicum of assurance that the project does not waste public resources and stem pork-barrel.

User Fee Finance
In Chapter 2, we emphasized the advantages of PVR contracts for high-demand projects that can pay for capital and operating expenses in all demand states. Many of the advantages of PVR contracts stem from the fact that they eliminate demand risk for the franchise holder, a desirable property because most of this risk is beyond the firm's control and often serves as an excuse for opportunistic renegotiations.

This section incorporates a second consideration for designing PPP contracts. We argue that, other things equal, financing infrastructure projects with user fees is less costly than financing them with government subsidies, where the latter includes a variety of means by which governments transfer resources to concessionaires, such as shadow fees, guarantees, and availability payments. User fees go directly into the concessionaire's pocket. Thus, by remunerating the concessionaire with user-fee revenue, society avoids the costs incurred from disbursing subsidies. These include standard overhead costs that are present in any organization, as well as the additional inefficiencies of government agencies: overstaffing, the lack of a board to pressure management to control overhead, the need to follow and comply with rigid administrative procedures and controls imposed by the budget and the comptroller's offices, and even the diversion of public funds and outright corruption.[8] Although many intuitions are quite general, the formal results we discuss next capture the advantage of user-fee finance over tax finance by assuming that the

---

[8] While a diversion of public funds might be a transfer, it usually involves wasteful activities and expenditures to conceal it. Furthermore, a diversion of $1 costs more than $1 because it is financed with distortionary taxation at the margin.

government has to disburse $1 + g$ dollars, with $g > 0$, to provide one dollar to the recipient.[9]

Consider projects with large demand uncertainty, with states that can pay for the project and others that cannot. We refer to these projects as *intermediate demand projects*, and reserve the term *low demand* to describe projects that cannot finance the upfront investment in any demand state. In intermediate demand projects, the government faces a trade-off between providing insurance and saving on costly subsidies.

The government can eliminate all demand risk for the franchise holder with an availability contract, at the cost of relying excessively on costly subsidies. A more efficient way of eliminating demand risk is via a straightforward extension of the PVR scheme. The project is auctioned to the firm asking for the lowest present value of revenues, and the government subsidizes any shortfall, thus ensuring that the winning firm collects its bid.[10]

This is inefficient because these resources need to go through the government bureaucracy, at a cost per unit of g, before they can be usefully spent. This suggests that allowing the concessionaire to collect more user fees in high-demand states may be better, even if this entails having the firm bear some risk and therefore charge a risk premium.

In Engel, Fischer, and Galetovic (2013), we show that fully insuring the concessionaire is not desirable for intermediate demand projects, and that the contract that optimally trades off costly subsidy finance against the firm's risk premium will reduce, but not eliminate, demand risk for the firm. The optimal contract combines a minimum revenue guarantee and a revenue cap. When demand realizations are low, the contract lasts indefinitely (or as long as the law allows), and the minimum income guarantee is binding, so that the government complements the concessionaire's income to attain the guaranteed level of revenues. When demand is high, the revenue cap sets in, and the contract ends when discounted revenue equals the cap. As in the case of a PVR contract, the franchise term is shorter in high-demand

---

[9] We assume there is no cost of collecting user fees. The results go through, with minor amendments, if the concessionaire's cost of collecting user fees is less than or equal to both the government's cost of collecting user fees and to the shadow cost of public funds.

[10] More specifically, assume there is a maximum concession length specified by law (much longer than the expected length of the concession). Each year, there is a schedule of expected revenues that add up to the winning bid. The government pays or recoups the difference between the expected revenues and the real revenues. If at the end of the maximum concession period the firm has not collected the value of its bid, the government pays over the difference.

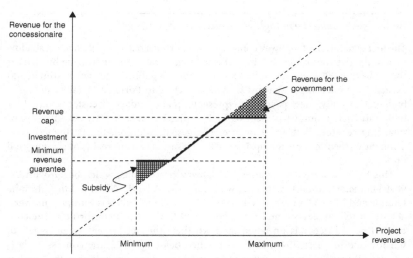

Figure 6.1 The optimal contract for an intermediate-demand road.

Figure 6.1 shows the optimal contract for an intermediate-demand road. If project revenues fall below the minimum revenue guarantee (low-demand states), the government subsidizes and covers the difference with project revenues. For intermediate-demand states, the concession lasts indefinitely, but the government does not subsidize. Last, in high-demand states, the concession ends when project revenues reach the revenue cap and the difference is cashed in by the government.

states. Figure 6.1 shows how subsidies and revenues vary with the project's discounted user fees for an intermediate demand project.

In low-demand states, the extension of PVR that fully insures the firm is optimal. In a low-demand project, it is optimal to provide subsidies in all states of demand. There are no states in which there is a trade-off between providing more revenue (and therefore saving on g) and increasing risk, as in the case of intermediate-demand projects. Because this trade-off is absent, the optimal contract minimizes subsidies and eliminates risk. As mentioned earlier, a social cost-benefit analysis is important for these projects to filter out white elephants. This is not surprising because low-demand projects, by definition, are not profitable without subsidies.

The first flexible-term highway concession in Europe has similarities with the optimal contract described earlier (see Box 6.4). The upside is limited via a revenue cap that applies after the concession reaches 22 years, while the downside risk is reduced by extending the concession to a maximum of 30 years.

Box 6.5 *A flexible-term highway concession in Portugal*

The first generation of highway concessions in Portugal began in 1999, using shadow tolls to finance the concessionaires. This led to a sizeable and increasing burden for the budget: in 2004, shadow toll obligations for the public sector were estimated to exceed €660 million per year by 2008, a sum close to Portugal's total annual road budget. Currently, these payments represent a major budgetary cost, reaching €1.1 billion in 2010, around 1 percent of GDP. It thus became attractive to shift toward financing schemes that relied on user charges. In addition, the Portuguese government wanted to limit the upside for the private sector on real (not shadow) toll projects.

This led to a second generation of highway concessions, which began with the 98.4-kilometer Litoral Centro highway along the Atlantic coast, linking Marinha Grande and Mira, at an estimated cost of €795 million. This was Europe's first variable-term toll concession and was adjudicated to the Brisal consortium. The concession period depends on when (and whether) the net present value (NPV) of toll revenue reaches €784 million. If reached before year 22, the concession lasts 22 years; if reached between years 22 and 30, the concession ends once this mark is attained; and if it has not been reached by year 30, the concession ends. Toll revenue is discounted using the 12-month Euribor rate, which provides a natural interest rate hedge: an increase in this rate reduces the NPV of toll revenues and therefore extends the concession term. The project benefits from annual toll increases in line with the Portuguese consumer price index.

The project won the Eurofinance prize for project of the year in 2004.[11] Even though the experience has been successful, the following highway PPPs in Portugal reverted to the fixed-term franchise model.[12] Note that because this contract involves no government subsidies, it provides stronger incentives to filter white elephants than the optimal contract for intermediate-demand projects, at the expense of excessive risk.[13] ∎

In Engel and colleagues (2013), we also show that the optimal contract can be implemented via a competitive auction with realistic informational requirements. The firms bid on both the toll revenue cap and on the minimum income guarantee, which are combined in a scoring function. These two thresholds differ in important ways from the minimum income guarantees and revenue-sharing agreements observed in practice. Minimum

---

[11] Based on *Project Finance* (2005).

[12] The Lusoponte (Vasco da Gama bridge over the river Tagus) contract of 1999 had a similar clause, but it was dropped during the first renegotiation of the contract. The Court of Audits (Tribunal de Contas) published a report criticizing that renegotiation, which it considered as "hurting the public interest," and valued that single variable-term clause at €500 million. Source: personal communication from Rui Monteiro.

[13] However, firms may still want to renegotiate the contract in the event of a bad outcome. This may explain why the Brisal consortium is suing the government for €1 billion, claiming that demand was lower than the official traffic forecasts.

income guarantees are routine in highway PPPs, but most real-world contracts have a fixed term and therefore do not follow the prescriptions laid out previously. These contracts would be closer to the optimal contract if their durations were longer in low-demand states, when guarantees are paid out. Thus, because of the fixed term length, real-world contracts pay excessive guarantees in low-demand states.

Real-world revenue-sharing agreements similarly do not coincide with the revenue cap that characterizes the optimal contract.[14] When governments impose revenue-sharing arrangements, they split revenues in excess of a given threshold with the concessionaire in fixed proportions. By contrast, the optimal contract described earlier suggests assigning all the revenue in excess of a given threshold to the government – the windfall profits tax rate should be 100 percent.

More generally, the rationale behind real-world guarantees and revenue-sharing schemes is to reduce the risk borne by the concessionaire. By contrast, the rationale behind the optimal contract is to optimally trade off insurance, on one hand, and the use of subsidies, on the other. This is why the concession lasts indefinitely when subsidies (that is, guarantees) are granted; the term is variable in high-demand states, and the concessionaire's revenue in high-demand states is higher than in low-demand states.

Two important assumptions are that demand is mainly exogenous and service quality is contractible. We illustrated the relevance of these assumptions in Chapter 3 (specifically in Section 3.3 and Box 3.1). If these assumptions do not hold and moral hazard plays an important role, the optimal contract may be similar to the one discussed earlier or it can be more complex, depending on the source of moral hazard. For example, if the concessionaire's effort can lead to a reduction in expected maintenance costs, a PVR auction will implement the optimal contract. The intuition is that the concessionaire will have more incentives to exert effort when demand realizations and revenues are low, so that any contribution to increased margins is more valuable. It follows that having firms bid for the least present value of revenues aligns incentives with the objective of building the project at the lowest cost.[15] By contrast, when demand responds to a large extent on unobservable actions by the concessionaire, the optimal contract is complex (see Engel et al. (2013) for details) and has stringent informational requirements.

---

[14] Profit-sharing agreements should be avoided because firms can (and do) use transfer pricing and other gimmicks to inflate their costs and thereby avoid sharing profits.

[15] For a formal proof, see Result 5 in the appendix.

6.4 Conclusion

There is no prima facie financial reason to prefer PPPs over public provision and PPPs never relax the constraints on public funds. Our conclusion rests on the observation that PPPs affect the discounted government budget in much the same way as public provision. With a PPP the current government saves in investment outlays. However, the government either relinquishes future user fee revenue (if the PPP is financed with user fees) or future tax revenues (if the PPP is financed with payments from the government budget). Not even credit-constrained governments are an exception. Hence, the case for PPPs must rest on something else, notably on efficiency gains associated with better incentives for maintenance or bundling of construction, maintenance, and operations, and not on their purported financial advantages.

From a public finance perspective, PPPs have disadvantages. Fiscal accounting rules keep most PPPs off the balance sheet, and governments have used them to anticipate spending and to sidestep the normal budgetary process, much in the same way that off-balance-sheet vehicles helped banks to elude capital requirements and prudential regulation with results that led to the financial crisis of 2008. This has been known for a long time, which suggests that incentives and political self-interest rather than ignorance are the reason for the lack of progress in improving PPP accounting rules. We conclude that, from the point of view of the government budget, PPPs should be treated as conventional government investment and should be included as public debt. While some claim that such a rule would reinforce the bias against capital spending present in public expenditures, we believe that experience so far – especially considering the fate of PPPs in a developed country such as the United Kingdom – makes it hard to believe that governments can be trusted to use off-balance-sheet vehicles wisely and prudently.

Bibliographic Notes

A comprehensive discussion of guarantees and fiscal risk is in Hemming (2006); see also Hemming (2008). On guarantees, see also Irwin (2007).

There is no agreement on whether and how to include PPPs in the public accounts and in the government's balance sheet. Useful contributions to this discussion are Heald (1997), Grimsey and Lewis (2002), and Donaghue (2002); see also Heald (2010) for an update on accounting and the PFI initiative and Heald and Georgiou (2011). Schwartz, Carbacho, and Funke

(2008, part four) contains several articles on accounting and PPPs. Eurotstat (2004) is perhaps the only systematic attempt to include PPPs in public accounts. See also the discussion of Eurostat in de Reugemont (2008).

A short but insightful discussion of the Ryrie Rules and of PPPs in general is Heald and McLeod (2002); see also Heald (1997). Maskin and Tirole (2008) is a theoretical study of how PPPs are used to elude spending limits. Engel, Fischer, and Galetovic (2009) show how renegotiations serve the same purpose.

Optimal risk-sharing contracts in PPPs have been studied by Engel, Fischer, and Galetovic (2001, 2013).

7

Renegotiations

A striking fact of PPP concessions is that they are routinely renegotiated. For example, Guasch (2004) examines nearly 1,000 Latin American concession contracts awarded between the mid-1980s and 2000; he finds that 54.4 percent of those in transportation (including roads, ports, tunnels, and airports) and 74.4 percent of those in the water industry had been renegotiated. When Mexico privatized highways in the late 1980s, Mexican taxpayers had to pay more than $8 billion (U.S. billion) after renegotiation of the initial contracts. In Chile, 47 out of the 50 Chilean PPP concessions awarded by the Ministry of Public Works between 1992 and 2005 had been renegotiated by 2006, and one of every four dollars invested had been obtained through renegotiation (see Engel et al., 2009).[1]

One might think that renegotiations occur mainly in emerging economies, where governance is weak. They are also pervasive in developed countries, however, as Gómez-Ibáñez and Meyer (1993) documented more than two decades ago. For example, three of the four highway concessions awarded in France in the early 1970s went bankrupt after the 1973 oil shock and were bailed out by the government. Similarly, several of the 12 highway concessions awarded in Spain in the 1970s had higher costs than anticipated, while traffic was lower than expected, causing three highways to go bankrupt and the remaining contracts to be renegotiated. Spain seems to be a serial subsidizer of PPPs at the expense of the public: in November 2010, all political parties agreed that it was necessary to bail out, among others, the seven PPP highways running into Madrid.[2]

---

[1] Bitrán (2011) reports that 63 percent of investment in PPPs in Colombia took place via renegotiations.

[2] See "Los partidos salvarán de la quiebra a las concesionarias de autopistas," *El País*, November 8, 2010.

Industry participants often claim that circumstances change over the life of a concession. Because most PPP contracts last for several decades, renegotiations of inherently incomplete contracts are to be expected. Renegotiations thus provide the flexibility necessary to adapt to changing conditions. While there is some truth to this argument, it ignores two disturbing features of most renegotiations. First, they often occur shortly after contracts are awarded. For example, Guasch finds that the average time to renegotiation was only 2.2 years after the concession was awarded, and 60 percent of all renegotiated contracts had been renegotiated within the first three years after the concession award (2004, p. 14). Our own research shows that 78 percent of the amounts awarded in renegotiations of PPPs in Chile were brokered during construction, shortly after the concession was awarded (Engel et al., 2009).

Second, renegotiations tend to favor the concessionaire. For example, Guasch (2004) finds that two-thirds led to tariff increases, 38 percent to extensions of the concession term, and two-thirds to reductions in investment obligations. In the case of Chilean PPPs, we find that most renegotiations imply paying more for the works than originally contracted. Thus, while in principle renegotiations may allow governments to expropriate concessionaires after they have sunk their investment, in practice it seems that the private partner benefits the most.

Contract renegotiation may be justifiable when the environment changes, new information arises, or design errors are discovered. In these cases, all parties, including the public, may gain from renegotiation. In other cases, however, the only reason to modify the contract is to favor either the procuring authority (in the case of expropriation of the PPP, for example) or the project sponsor (by helping a failing project, offering a term extension, or lowering the technical standards) – or both these parties at the expense of users or taxpayers. In practice, it is difficult to discriminate between justifiable and unjustifiable renegotiations. Even when renegotiations are justified, the resulting agreement may not be fair, given that renegotiations occur in a situation of bilateral monopoly.

Still, renegotiations that benefit the concessionaire and increase its profits do not necessarily create rents, provided that the concession is awarded by competitive bidding. In a competitive auction, any potential transfer of rents to the concessionaire ex post should be dissipated ex ante in the competition for the concession. We argue, however, that even under competitive auctions, renegotiations cause inefficiencies.

7.1 Accounting and Spending Anticipation

An inefficiency caused by renegotiations is that, just as in the case of minimum revenue guarantees and PPPs in general, they allow incumbent
governments to elude budgetary spending and debt limits and thus lead
to excessive current spending on infrastructure. Under public provision,
caps on spending or net fiscal debt are reasonably effective in controlling
this bias because additional expenditures established in contract renegotiations must be included in the budget. By contrast, given that fiscal
accounting standards are defective, renegotiations of PPP contracts can
be used to elude spending caps. Essentially, because PPPs bundle finance
and construction, the firm can "lend" to the government by renegotiating the contract in return for payments made by future administrations.
Under current fiscal accounting rules, neither the additional investments
brokered in renegotiations nor the future obligations assumed by the government are counted in the budget. This suggests that the solution to the
spending bias is the same as the solution discussed for PPPs in general:
any additions to the project should be considered capital expenditures and
therefore counted as debt.

If the anticipation of spending through renegotiations is a real problem,
the prediction is that one should observe the following. First, firms would
lowball their offers, expecting to recover their contractual losses through
renegotiations. Second, additional works would be included when contracts
are renegotiated. Third, major renegotiations would occur shortly after the
award of the contract, during construction. Fourth, an important fraction
of the costs of renegotiation would be borne by future administrations.
While there is little systematic data on renegotiations, we have compiled
information on the 50 PPP concessions awarded in Chile between 1993
and 2006 (Engel, Fischer, and Galetovic, 2009, and Engel et al., 2009). Total
investment increased via renegotiation from $8.4 billion to $11.3 billion,
that is, by nearly one-third. Most of the increase (83 percent of the total)
was the result of 78 bilateral renegotiations, while the rest was the result
of decisions of arbitration panels. For the $2.3 billion awarded in bilateral
renegotiations, the administration that renegotiated paid only 35 percent
of the additional cost. Moreover, 84 percent corresponds to payments for
additional works, while the remaining 16 percent corresponds to additional
payments for works included in the original contract. Of the total, 78 percent was awarded during the construction phase. Finally, even though specific provisions in the Chilean concessions law limit the amounts that can
be renegotiated, these limits are routinely exceeded.

7.2 Adverse Selection and Moral Hazard

Adverse Selection and Renegotiations

Pervasive renegotiations attract firms that are better (re)negotiators and skilled at lobbying, corrupting officials, and rallying public support. As mentioned briefly in Section 1.1, these firms will tend to be technically less efficient because of competitive selection. The economics is as follows. Because renegotiations between the concessionaire and the government are bilateral, surpluses are split according to the relative bargaining abilities of each. A better lobbyist should get a larger fraction of the pie in any renegotiation. Hence, if two firms are equally efficient, but one hires a better lobbyist, the one with the better lobbyist has an edge in the auction for the project. Under competition for government contracts, firms that are worse in both their technical efficiency and their ability to renegotiate will not survive – they cannot compensate for lower technical efficiency with the possibility of higher revenue from renegotiation. It follows that the firm with the highest degree of technical efficiency will also employ less skillful renegotiators because they will not have to renegotiate to compensate for inefficiency. The implication is that if a substantial part of profits are made in the renegotiation stage, less efficient firms will have an advantage. Hence by self-selection, efficient firms should be attracted to countries in which there is little renegotiation of the initial contract, while countries that renegotiate will attract technically less advanced firms.

The remedy to this adverse selection problem is to eliminate the possibility of economic rents in contract renegotiations. This would require that any changes do not increase the payment for contracted services – the so-called sanctity-of-the-bid principle (Guasch, 2004). However, additional investments that are required to provide higher standards of service should be put to competitive tender, ensuring that the concessionaire does not obtain rents in a bilateral renegotiation. In that case, the concessionaire's lobbying power is irrelevant, so any advantage in the original bidding stage vanishes, and there is no adverse selection against technical efficiency.

Moral Hazard and Renegotiations

PPPs are appropriate when objective quality standards can be set, measured, and enforced. In that case, the concessionaire can be left to choose the production technology, and the cost-cutting incentives will be equivalent to those under a fixed-price contract or a price cap. In practice, however, concessionaires promote the belief that PPP contracts should be adjusted to secure the financial equilibrium of the concessionaire, an argument that firms often produce to justify renegotiations (among many examples, this was the case for the recent bailout of Spanish PPPs).

This is not an acceptable argument for a renegotiation of the contract. If the firm's bids were prudent, the company should expect to receive the normal return on investment after adjusting for risk, as in all other sectors of the economy. Hence, the sanctity of the bid should be preserved, and there should be no renegotiation if there are increases in the cost of providing the contracted service quality.

Renegotiations are not only unnecessary, but also inefficient, because they weaken the incentives to control and reduce costs, thereby dampening the advantages of bundling. Renegotiations meant to restore the concessionaire's financial equilibrium transform a fixed-price contract into a cost-plus contract thereby reducing incentives to contain costs. Even worse, because firms with strong renegotiation skills can extract more from the government, they can afford to exert even less effort to control costs. Thus, moral hazard increases the advantage good renegotiators hold even further and worsens the adverse selection problem.

When the PPP agency has discretion to renegotiate, it feels less pressure to plan and design projects carefully, because it can renegotiate away its own mistakes. The problem is compounded when the costs of renegotiating can be shifted to future administrations and when the PPP agency is not accountable. Thus, when coupled with inadequate accounting or governance, the expectation of renegotiations generates moral hazard in the PPP agency.

Finally, easy renegotiations lower the risk of failure, which may help attract lenders. For the same reason, renegotiations weaken the market test that competitive auctions would provide for concessions that can pay their way with user fees. If contracts are renegotiated whenever the concessionaire stands to lose, firms will not mind building white elephants. The only market test that PPPs provide becomes irrelevant.

7.3 Flexibility and Renegotiation

Circumstances change over the life of a long-term contract. If demand grows faster than expected, the PPP facility may need to be enlarged before the current concession ends; or if the original user fee schedule proves inadequate, it may become desirable to change it. In those cases, one would like to grant the regulator flexibility to change the contract and, perhaps, even to terminate it unilaterally. This would facilitate regulatory takings, however, so many contract clauses restrict discretion to protect concessionaires.

The tension between protecting the concessionaire from regulatory takings and avoiding the costs of inflexibility can be illustrated with two recent U.S. PPP road concessions. In 1995, the California Department of Transportation (Caltrans) awarded a 35-year concession for a 10-mile segment of the four-lane Riverside Freeway (also called State Route 91) between the Orange-Riverside county line and the Costa Mesa Freeway (State Route 55) to a private firm, California Private Transportation Corporation (CPTC). Motorists used the express lanes to avoid congestion in the non-tolled lanes, paying up to almost $11 for a round trip. The concessionaire was allowed to raise tolls to relieve congestion, which it did several times. By the late 1990s, 33,000 daily trips brought the express lanes to the brink of congestion at peak time, turning the concession into a financial success. At the same time and for the same reasons, users in the non-tolled public lanes were suffering congestion, and an expansion was urgently needed. Nevertheless, the contract included a non-compete clause that prevented Caltrans from raising capacity at Riverside Freeway without CPTC's consent during the 35 years of the concession. Caltrans tried to go around the clause, arguing that expansions were necessary to prevent accidents, but CPTC filed a lawsuit. The settlement stated that non-compete clauses were meant to ensure the financial viability of CPTC and that they restrict Caltrans's right to adversely affect the project's traffic or revenues. Consequently, no new lanes could be built.

Protracted negotiations ensued, and eventually the Orange County Transportation Authority (OCTA) was empowered to negotiate the purchase of the tolled lanes. Unfortunately, the value of the toll road was controversial because, strictly speaking, it should have been the present value of profits from the State Route 91 Express Lanes had the franchise continued as originally planned. Although the lanes cost $130 million to build, initially the company's value was set at $274 million in a controversial (and ultimately unsuccessful) attempt at a buyout by a nonprofit associated with Orange County. After several years of negotiations, with frustrated commuters stuck in traffic in the meantime, the express lanes were bought in January 2003 by OCTA for $207.5 million. The purchase was enabled by the California legislature, which gave the OCTA the authority to collect tolls and pay related financing costs and also eliminated non-compete provisions in the franchise agreement to allow for needed improvements on State Route 91.

The non-compete clause was clearly inefficient ex post, and it might seem that Caltrans made a mistake by including it in the original contract. This type of inflexibility may be justified, however, as illustrated by the 14-mile

Dulles Greenway Highway, which was designed as a BOT facility that would become the property of the State of Virginia after 42.5 years.

Virginia's General Assembly authorized the private development of toll roads in 1988. A group of investors thought that a toll road linking Washington's Dulles International Airport and Leesburg, Virginia, would be a promising investment. Their expectations were based on the prospect of residential and commercial growth in the area, which was causing increased congestion on existing arterial roads serving the corridor. To finance the Greenway, investors put up $40 million in cash and secured $310 million in privately placed taxable debt. Loans were to be repaid with toll revenues. Investors underestimated how much users dislike paying tolls, and initial revenues were much lower than forecast. Moreover, investors did not count on the State of Virginia widening the congested Route 7, which serves the same users. As mentioned in Chapter 3, two independent consulting companies had predicted that when the road opened in 1996, with an average toll of $1.75, there would be a daily flow of 35,000 vehicles. In practice, however, the average number of vehicles per day turned out to be only 8,500, just one-fourth of the initial estimates. After tolls were lowered to $1.00, ridership increased to 23,000, still far below predictions. The bonds that were issued to finance the project were renegotiated, and some of the original investors wrote off their equity. After refinancing and an extension of the franchise term to 60 years, the project became financially viable.

In principle, the government should be able to unilaterally buy back the concession, provided that it pays a fair compensation for the profits forgone by the franchise holder – that is, the expected present value of future profits had the concession continued under the original terms. The problem is that with a fixed-term concession, like Orange County's State Route 91, this amount cannot be deduced from accounting data and is highly subjective. Neither discretion nor bilateral bargaining leads to an efficient solution.

As shown in Chapter 6.3, the optimal contract (namely, a PVR in the case of user fees and an availability contract otherwise) shifts exogenous demand risk away from the concessionaire. Furthermore, the optimal contract can be structured so that the government retains almost full flexibility, while the concessionaire is protected against arbitrary takings. For example, in the case of PVR, it suffices to add a clause allowing the regulator to buy out the franchise by paying the difference between the winning bid and the discounted value of collected toll revenue at the time of repurchase (minus a simple estimate of savings in maintenance and operations expenditures due to early termination). The compensation in the case of an availability contract is similar. In both cases the government bears the risk of early termination, which is desirable because this risk is beyond the concessionaire's control (see Chapter 4).

In contrast to a fixed-term concession, the compensation the concessionaire receives at termination under PVR is independent of future demand and is therefore verifiable. Thus, the winning bid minus the payments already received by the concessionaire always equals the fair compensation. In this case, the government cancels the contract only if doing so is efficient. Because the government can cancel the contract at its discretion, renegotiations are no longer protracted or inefficient.

7.4 Renegotiation and Contracting

Given the leeway that PPP agencies usually have, they will almost inevitably renegotiate their contracts to anticipate spending or correct their mistakes. Such incentives can be corrected with proper governance, which subjects projects and renegotiations to external review and approval (see the next chapter). Nevertheless, improvements in governance are not sufficient to deter renegotiations. In the usual fixed-term PPPs, revenues depend on exogenous demand, which is likely to be inefficient (see Chapter 6). It also increases the likelihood of pressures to renegotiate the contract by creating circumstances in which the concessionaire suffers losses. Concessionaires often expect to be bailed out at the time they make their bids for the project. More generally, as Guasch points out, firms in regulated industries expect their revenues to ensure reasonable profits (the principle of financial equilibrium), and they feel entitled to change the contract terms to prevent losses (2004, p. 35).

The frequency of renegotiations can be reduced by using variable-term contracts when user fees are the source of revenues. Similarly, when the payments come from the government, availability payments should replace shadow tolls. As mentioned in Chapter 3, in a fixed-term franchise, revenues are variable and depend on demand realizations. Hence, if the concession is assigned in a competitive auction, there will be demand realizations under which the concessionaire loses money, even though on average the concession obtains normal returns. By shifting demand risk from the concessionaire to the state, variable-term contracts or PPPs with availability payments reduce the states of demand that generate big losses, which is when concessionaires demand a renegotiation of the contract (see Chapter 3.3).

Fixed-term contracts have additional features that increase the likelihood of renegotiations. First, compensations must be based on revenue projections, which are subjective because they depend on demand and cost forecasts. Second, under fixed-term concessions, opportunistic renegotiations usually result in higher user fees or an extension of the contract, both of which are difficult to value. By contrast, under a PVR contract, higher user fees lead to the earlier end of the franchise, with no other effect on the revenues of the firm. Second, under variable-term and availability contracts, the winning bid reveals the revenue that the concessionaire expected in order to obtain a normal rate of profit. The existence of an objective benchmark serves as a deterrent for opportunistic renegotiations, because it is easier to value the transfer to the concessionaire that results from the renegotiation process. This helps the government resist pressures in favor of opportunistic renegotiations.

Under these optimal contracts, demand realizations do not affect revenues, so the bids become cost oriented (Tirole, 1997). When contracts transfer demand risk to the state, the concessionaire stabilizes its revenues, and losses are due to excessive costs in building, operations, and maintenance.

7.5 Conclusion

As we argued in Chapter 4, cost risk should be borne by the concessionaire, as long as the contractual service standards remain unchanged. A prudent bid should lead to financial equilibrium ex ante, and there should not be a renegotiation if costs turn out to be higher than expected. In other words, the principle of financial equilibrium should be explicitly abandoned.[3] The notion of financial equilibrium distorts incentives and is inconsistent with one of the main promises of PPPs, namely, the cost-efficient delivery of infrastructure services.

Of course, the government may decide to raise service standards or may want to enlarge infrastructure facilities. If additional investments and improved service standards are needed, the concessionaire has to be compensated. These additional investments should be included in the current debt to avoid the use of PPPs to circumvent budgetary controls and anticipate spending. Whenever possible, these additional investments should also be tendered in competitive auctions, and revenues should be raised only to the level required to restore the normal return on additional investments. This helps avoid opportunistic renegotiations and the advantage they provide to firms with a comparative advantage in lobbying over their technical

---

[3] This is easier if the governance of PPPs is improved by a separation of roles, as argued in Chapter 8.

efficiency. This requires that any renegotiation be subject to independent review, a topic we discuss in the next chapter.

Bibliographic Notes

The first comprehensive empirical study of renegotiations of PPPs came from Guasch (2004), who analyzed more than 1,000 concession contracts in Latin America and established several stylized facts that we discuss in this chapter. Several theoretical and empirical papers followed from this book. Guasch, Laffont, and Straub (2006) develop a theory of the determinants of renegotiations. Guasch, Laffont, and Straub (2007) apply the theory to quantify the determinants of government-led renegotiations in Latin America. Guasch, Laffont, and Straub (2008) empirically study renegotiations in transport and water in Latin America. Guasch and Straub (2006), Andres, Guasch, and Straub (2007), and Andres and Guasch (2008) are shorter and useful overviews of this line of research.

Engel, Fischer, and Galetovic (2009) analyze the link between spending anticipation, lowballing, and renegotiations. Their paper also provides systematic evidence from Chile's PPP program (see also Engel et al., 2009). Athias and Nuñez (2008, 2009) find evidence that concessionaires bid more aggressively when the likelihood of a renegotiation is higher.

A simple model of renegotiations and flexibility can be found in Engel, Fischer, and Galetovic (2003). The trade-off between opportunism and renegotiation is analyzed by Chong, Huet, and Saussier (2006) and Athias and Saussier (2010). Estache and others (2009) examine how choosing multiple criteria to award PPPs in auctions stimulates renegotiations. Guasch and Straub (2009) analyze the link between corruption and renegotiations. Last, de Brux (2010) discusses renegotiations and long-term relationships.

8

Governance

In this chapter, we look at the governance of the public works authority (PWA). We argue that PPPs share some of the same defects as standard public works, related to improper project design, selection, and opportunistic renegotiations. Because these problems are due to failures of governance in PWAs, our analysis leads to recommendations to address these weaknesses.[1] We explore some issues specifically related to the governance of PPPs, but our recommendations are applicable to the governance structure of the PWA in general.

8.1 Why PPPs Need Good Governance

When delivering infrastructure, governments face three challenges: first, deciding what and when to build; second, building it cost effectively; and third, ensuring proper maintenance and service quality thereafter. Governments in general have been unsuccessful at meeting these challenges. In many countries, infrastructure facilities include white elephants or earmarks directed at particular political constituencies; pricing is inefficient; there is X-inefficiency and lack of innovation and technological advance. Because resources are limited, these projects are built at the expense of socially worthwhile projects. It is not unusual for infrastructure procurement to be opaque and even corrupt, and the PWA is often biased against maintenance spending. Heggie and Vickers describe the reason for these shortcomings in the case of roads, but their description is applicable to most types of infrastructure:

---

[1] These proposals were motivated by some of the reforms of the Chilean Concessions Law and of the Public Works Secretariat discussed in recent years. See Bitrán and Villena (2010).

[Roads] are not managed as part of the market economy with its formidable pricing dynamic. There is no clear price for roads, road expenditures are most often financed from general tax revenues, and the road agency is not subjected to any rigorous market discipline. These bias managerial incentives. Roads are managed like a social service with multiple goals. Road users pay taxes and user charges, but the proceeds are almost always treated as general tax revenues. Instead of being financed through user charges, roads are thus financed through budget allocations determined as part of the annual budgetary process. These allocations bear little relationship to underlying needs ... or to users' willingness to pay. There is no direct link between revenues and expenditures, no price to ration demand ..., and expenditures are not subjected to the rigorous tests of the marketplace. (1998, p. 19)

In other words, many of the defects of public infrastructure provision stem from the absence of real prices, let alone competitive markets. On the supply side, the PPP unit is not rewarded according to project performance. This agency pursues multiple objectives and serves multiple principals. On the demand side, there is a disconnection between the availability of an infrastructure facility and users' willingness to pay.

When PPPs started to become common, the belief was that private participation by itself would correct these deficiencies. In retrospect, this view was naïve. PPPs do not release governments from their planning obligations. On the contrary, governments continue to plan and coordinate network expansion as demand grows over time, given that PPPs are associated with individual projects with temporary contracts. This means that, as in the more general case of public provision of infrastructure, the end result depends on the ability to select good public projects. Another erroneous belief was that there is a market test, at least in the case of projects that were financed with user fees. However, revenue guarantees are pervasive and frequent contract renegotiations in PPPs nullify the market test. In addition, many PPP projects require subsidies or do not charge user fees, so they never face this test.

As mentioned earlier, the ubiquity of contract renegotiations casts doubts on the real efficiencies of PPPs. In Chapter 7 we showed that technically inefficient firms have a competitive advantage when renegotiations are routine (the adverse selection problem). Routine renegotiations also weaken the incentives of the PPP unit to be careful in the design and selection of projects, and reduce the pressure on firms to cut costs (the moral hazard problem).

Finally, while the bundling associated with PPPs leads to better maintenance and the minimization of life-cycle costs, a public agency is needed to monitor and enforce standards. This is only possible when measurable standards can be defined and enforced. When service quality is not contractible, however, the private party may trade off quality against lower costs. In these cases, it is necessary to grant the public agency some degree of discretion (beyond what can be written in a formal contract) so that it can enforce appropriate standards.

In sum, markets do not provide a substitute for the proper governance of the PPP unit. First, many infrastructure services are financed with availability payments or receive subsidies, so they face no meaningful market test. Second, when user fees pay for infrastructure services, most facilities are natural monopolies, so concessionaires feel no competitive pressure. This means that regulatory governance is a key determinant of performance. In the next section, we describe the defects of current PPP governance and present proposals for reform.

8.2 PPPs and Governance: Practice

The governance structure under which most PPPs operate is usually defective. There are two main reasons: the first relates to PPPs in particular, while the second relates to defects in the governance structure of infrastructure procurement more generally. In many countries, PPPs were regarded as little more than an additional contractual form for project delivery, so they were embedded within existing agencies and their regulation was an adaptation of existing regulations. Because PPP projects are delivered on an individual basis, they have been regulated by their contract, and practitioners have seen little need to set up a specific governance structure. Finally, PPP stakeholders have little interest in setting up a better regulatory framework for PPPs, in part because the example could also lead to reforms in the governance of public provision, which would affect them directly.

More generally, as with all works of public infrastructure, PPPs suffer from their attractiveness to politicians, who value inaugurating new facilities. Politicians also favor concentrated and local interests and care less about quality of service and routine maintenance. Similarly, construction firms that specialize in working with the public sector prefer opaque arrangements that exclude entrants and are skilled at renegotiating contracts. Finally, sectorial authorities are biased toward the development of new projects and find that strict oversight and regulation works against that objective.

Perhaps the most glaring organizational defect in most PPP units is that a single institution is responsible for all aspects of the production and delivery cycle: the planning, tendering, construction, maintenance, supervision, contract enforcement, and conflict resolution. Conflicts of interest are inevitable under this governance structure. For example, if mistakes are made during the planning or design stage, the authority has every incentive to renegotiate the contract behind closed doors (thus leaving the concessionaire in a strong bargaining position). In turn this fosters careless design of projects.

Similarly, the PPP unit is often intent on additional building, and it therefore neglects the maintenance of existing infrastructure, preferring to sacrifice the latter in the interests of the former. Agencies in charge of PPPs tend to replicate this unitary structure (and are usually embedded within the PWA), so they are afflicted with similar problems.

A second defect of public provision is that agencies, ministries, and their internal departments tend to be organized by product and not by function. For example, across the government, often a department within the Health Ministry builds and operates hospitals, a separate department in the Ministry of Education is in charge of new school construction, and a department at the Ministry of Public Works builds new roads. These departments make plans with little or no coordination, seldom report to a central infrastructure agency, and often execute projects independently. While decentralization by product has some merit, there is also a need for cross-sector coordination. Ultimately, all public projects compete with each other through the government's budget constraint. This means that it is essential to have independent evaluation and formal approval of infrastructure projects to achieve efficient investment decisions.

In some countries, the governance of PPPs improves on the traditional model of infrastructure provision. Within Chile's PWA, for example, the agency responsible for PPPs covers all infrastructure areas, including those belonging to other ministries. By contrast, under the traditional system, the Ministry of Public Works has separate divisions for airports, roads, water reservoirs, and so on. Nevertheless, the Chilean PPP unit seldom coordinates its investments with other departments within the PWA, and infrastructure units within the separate ministries seldom coordinate their investments with the PPP unit.

According to Liu (2011), China has dealt with this problem with special purpose infrastructure companies. For example, in Shanghai, one urban development and investment corporation (UDIC), the Shanghai Chentou UDIC, is in charge of infrastructure such as subways, bridges, power, and water. This public company can enter PPP contracts with private providers through a subsidiary.

Last, PPP projects are rarely subject to cost-benefit evaluations by an independent central agency that supervises public investments and has the power to stop projects that do not pass the hurdle rate. As we showed in Chapter 6, PPP projects have the same effect on the discounted government budget as publicly provided infrastructure, which confirms the need to subject them to the same cost-benefit evaluations and rules as standard public projects. PPPs have done little to bring coherence to the overall plan of public investments, especially in the case of unsolicited offers (see Section 4.3). Moreover, even self-financing PPPs may create positive or negative externalities, which should be considered when assessing the desirability of a project.

8.3 A Proposal for PPP Governance

Our thesis in this book is that PPPs have the potential to improve the provision of infrastructure services. To achieve these potential gains, it is essential to ameliorate the regulatory governance of PPPs and of the PWA more generally. Our ambitious proposal consists of four interrelated aspects: (i) the PPP unit should be restricted to project planning, design, and delivery; (ii) projects should be subject to social cost-benefit evaluation by a unit that is independent of the PWA and then reviewed and approved by an independent PPP board; (iii) an independent PPP superintendence should supervise compliance with the PPP contract; and (iv) an independent expert panel should review renegotiations and arbitrate conflicts. This proposal addresses the enormous pressures bought to bear on the PPP unit (or more generally on the delivery unit of traditionally procured infrastructure) by setting up checks and balances at the stages of project approval, delivery, and use.

Under our proposal, the PPP unit's core business is to deliver socially valuable infrastructure. The PPP unit relinquishes control once the project is operational, and no longer monitors compliance with the contract. Within the PPP unit, a planning and design department should be in charge of conceiving new projects. This department should be in close contact with the different ministries and government agencies to ensure that these projects respond to real needs. The department should also know the PPP industry well and have a clear grasp of what is feasible. The planning and design department should work closely with the departments within the PPP unit that are in charge of project tendering and delivery.

The cost-benefit evaluation should be centralized within an agency that oversees all public investments. Political interference can be reduced if the evaluation division is sufficiently independent and if projects must pass a hurdle rate to be eligible, thereby eliminating earmarks and white elephants.

Hence, this division should have sufficient standing to withstand the pressures of politicians.

Having a social evaluation filter should improve the quality of public investment (and therefore PPPs). For sufficiently large projects, additional improvements are possible if, after the social evaluation stage, the project is reviewed by a high-level board with the authority to approve it, to ask for modifications, or to reject the project. This board should go beyond the cost-benefit analysis and assess the overall feasibility of the project, its interaction with other projects, the project's business plan, user fee levels, and sources of financing, especially when subsidies are necessary. In addition, the board should approve any substantial modifications or additions to the project (before the revisions are sent to the panel for valuation). After approval by the board, the contract should be tendered competitively. Tenders and contracts should be drafted by a specialized department within the PPP unit and approved by the board. To perform its role, the board should be politically and financially independent. Members should be chosen for their skills and professional standing, and they should bear responsibility for their decisions, as do members of a corporate board.

After a private firm or concessionaire wins the contract, compliance becomes an issue, and independent supervision is required. We propose that a PPP superintendence – a unit independent of the PPP unit – should monitor contract compliance. This is essential to break the conflict of interest between promotion of new investment and strict supervision of contracts. Because the superintendence has an undivided mandate, it will be more likely to enforce the PPP contract.

The PPP unit should remain in charge of the project while the concessionaire builds the new facility and until the infrastructure is delivered and becomes operational. The reason is that the PPP unit is in the business of delivering infrastructure and should have firsthand experience of operational difficulties. Moreover, while planning, design, and tendering are essential, they should be subordinated to delivery. In other words, the PPP unit should bear responsibility for delivering the project. The superintendence should simultaneously monitor the process of construction.

Finally, there should be a formal mechanism for conflict resolution. Conflicts between the concessionaire and the PPP unit or the superintendence should be arbitrated by an independent panel of experts. The panel should also review contract renegotiations, during both construction and operation of the project, with a view to keeping the net present value of the project to the private firm unchanged (thus reducing incentives to renegotiate). This panel should be independent, and it should base its decisions on technical, judicial, and economic considerations. Panel members should be hired for their skills and professional standing.

8.4 Conclusion

Our proposals are ambitious and probably face too much opposition to be achieved in the short run. Nevertheless, partial improvements are achievable: each one of these aspects, if implemented alone, could improve on the present situation.

Bibliographic Notes

Chapter 8 in Grimsey and Lewis (2004b) discusses the governance of PPPs. Chapter 5 in OECD (2008) describes the role that PPP units can play in infrastructure provision; Chapter 6 discusses the regulation of PPPs.

Saussier, Staropoli, and Yvrande-Billon (2009) discuss the impact of institutional weaknesses on public-private agreements' performance. Estache and colleagues (2009) show evidence that good governance moderates renegotiations. The study by the Economist Intelligence Unit (2009) is an interesting evaluation of institutional strength and weaknesses in Latin America.

9

When and How to Implement PPPs

This book seeks to answer three questions: When are PPPs the best way to provide and finance infrastructure? How should PPP contracts be designed? What is the appropriate governance structure for PPPs? The answers depend on the type of infrastructure facility and on the institutional conditions in the country (or municipality, state, or province) in question. Nevertheless, several guiding principles emerge from the material we have covered in this book. In this final chapter we take stock of the various issues and speculate about the future of public-private partnerships.

9.1 When to Use PPPs

Institutions

In this book, we have defined a PPP as an arrangement by which a private firm (the concessionaire, usually a special purpose vehicle or SPV) sinks a substantial upfront investment to build, revamp, or acquire an existing infrastructure facility that provides services to the public. As repayment for the capital, maintenance, and operating costs, the firm receives user fee revenues, government transfers, or a combination of both during the life of a long-term contract. At the end of the concession the facility is returned to the state.

The concessionaire's expenses are front loaded, while revenue collection is back loaded. This cash flow stream can only be attractive to private firms if they are reasonably confident that revenue streams will not be expropriated, that is, if the rules of law and property rights are strong. If regulatory takings or expropriations are likely, only less risky, traditional public provision of infrastructure facilities is possible because in that case the firm is paid earlier in the life of the infrastructure, on the basis of completed work.

This basic insight suggests that PPPs are unattractive for most low-income countries with weak institutions.

Do PPPs Free Public Funds?

Most arguments in favor of PPPs stress that they release public funds, which the government can spend elsewhere. As we have shown, however, a PPP affects the intertemporal government budget in much the same way as public provision: with a PPP the current government saves the initial investment outlay. But then it either relinquishes future user fee revenue (if the PPP is financed with user fees) or future spending (if the PPP is financed with payments from the government budget). Indeed, we have argued that, from the point of view of their fiscal impact, PPPs should be treated much like public projects.

Efficiency and PPPs

Because there is no prima facie financial reason to prefer PPPs over public provision, their case must stand or fall on the potential efficiency gains that they can achieve. While few empirical studies estimate the efficiency gains of PPPs, the prejudice in their favor is warranted.

One reason is organizational. Public agencies in charge of infrastructure projects (for example, ministries of public works) tend to have multiple objectives, are accountable to multiple principals, and have goals that are set as part of the political process. Moreover, it is difficult to link pay and performance in the public sector, public agencies are constrained by the annual budget cycle, and, possibly for good reasons, management practices in the public sector are more rigid than in the private sector. Finally, because a ministry or public agency manages a large number of projects, scale and scope are likely to be well beyond what is efficient. All this suggests that incentives will be blunted.

PPPs are the opposite type of organization. Each project is managed by a different SPV and their focus is narrow. Moreover, SPVs are private firms unconstrained by public sector rigidities and their goal is private gain. Thus workers' pay can be linked to performance and endogenous risks can be transferred to the responsible agents, thereby mitigating moral hazard. Last, a long-term contract isolates the SPV from the year-to-year vagaries of the public budget. All this suggests that incentives are more powerful under a PPP. To the extent that more powerful incentives foster efficiency, this is an argument in favor of PPPs.

A second reason is that PPPs financed with user fees may contribute further to efficiency. In principle, competitive auctions can be used to filter white elephants. Moreover, it tends to be easier to charge tolls when the infrastructure is privately provided, and user fees allow governments to reduce distortionary taxation. Lastly, user fees substitute for subsidies. The latter are more expensive than the former because agency problems in the public sector lead to rigidities in public expenditures that make it more expensive to transfer a dollar to the concessionaire via subsidies than via tolls. This cost can be compounded by inefficiencies and corruption in the public works authority.

A final reason is that long-term contracts can improve maintenance, in many countries one of the main shortcomings of traditional provision. In theory, governments could set aside the resources needed to maintain the infrastructure at the time of building. In practice, they tend to prefer to build new projects and spend on maintenance only when the facility has deteriorated. This stop-and-go approach is more expensive than timely maintenance – for example, a tripling of maintenance costs is common in the case of highways. Under a PPP, an SPV is bound by contract to maintain the facility according to predefined standards, and continuous maintenance is usually optimal for the concessionaire.

Privatization versus PPPs
Most of the efficiency gains PPPs bring about seem to arise from "privatizing" the infrastructure. Why not go all the way? One reason is politics – in many countries privatization faces opposition and PPPs seem to be a feasible second best. More fundamentally, PPPs are more convenient when the scope of planning exceeds individual projects. For example, most individual roads are part of a wider network, but the owner of one private road does not have incentives to internalize network-wide externalities that need to be addressed over long time periods. Unless the government maintains planning control, this constrains its ability to further develop the network and to adjust plans to changing needs and circumstances. A similar problem emerges with landlord ports where port facilities must be planned by one entity but terminals can be operated by different firms.

The PPP Premium
Observed financing costs for PPPs are higher than for government debt – experts claim that the so-called PPP premium is between 200 and 300 basis points. It is sometimes argued that unless a PPP produces efficiency gains at least as large as the premium, traditional provision should be preferred. We find this argument unconvincing.

One reason is that the risk a bondholder bears under public provision is subsumed under general government default risk. Governments could borrow money even for useless purposes and the rate on government debt would not increase significantly because lenders look only at the level of global indebtedness and do not evaluate individual projects.

Part of the observed PPP premium may be due to inappropriate contracting. Fixed-term concessions that allocate exogenous demand risk to the concessionaire command a premium that can be avoided with flexible-term contracts. To the extent that firms have a harder time diversifying exogenous risk than governments, this suggests that forcing the concessionaire to bear exogenous demand risk will result in higher borrowing costs for no good reason.

Finally, one of the main points of a PPP is to shift endogenous risk to the concessionaire to prevent moral hazard and to strengthen incentives to cut costs and provide adequate service quality. Unless the concessionaire is risk neutral, he will charge for bearing that risk. Moreover, these risks are not diversifiable in the capital market for if they could be diversified, there would be no incentive to improve performance in the first place. The "right" PPP pemium would compare financing costs under public provision, coupled to an incentive contract where the agent bears endogenous risk, with the financing costs under a PPP. In practice, however, the inability to make remunerations depend on performance means that traditional provision cannot transfer endogenous risks to agents.

When and When Not To Use PPPs

PPPs are not always better than public provision. Research has identified the basic trade-off: other things equal, PPPs stimulate investments that cut life-cycle costs and actions that lower costs in general, but costs can be cut at the expense of service quality and user welfare. Thus, whether a PPP is the best alternative depends on project characteristics. They are likely to work better than public provision when objective quality standards can be defined, measured, and enforced, or when users observe quality and can use their voice to press for better service. By contrast, public provision is the preferred organizational form when quality is the main concern and is not contractible.

The problem is fundamental for many public services. To define "objective" standards one must translate goals into a measurable scale. This is easy to do with roads or ports, where performance standards are agreed upon and can be enforced. But it may be very hard (or even impossible) when services are complex and goals are ambiguous, as in the case of education, health, jails, and information technology services. Not surprising, in many of these cases results with PPPs have been mixed at best.

Summing up, PPPs are likely to do better than the traditional approach to infrastructure provision when long-term contracts do not expose the firm to significant expropriation risk, service quality is contractible at low cost, and privatization is unattractive or unfeasible. In this case PPPs may be viewed as the preferred option, in the sense that the institutional challenges that must be addressed are likely to be less daunting than those needed to improve the traditional model.

9.2 How to Design and Implement PPPs

Contract Design

Project finance has emerged as a financing technique well suited for PPP projects by allowing the project's sponsor – an equity investor responsible for bidding, developing, and managing the project – to borrow against the cash flow of a project that is legally and economically self-contained. Project finance has clear advantages over corporate finance. During the construction phase, the stand-alone nature of the SPV precludes underinvestment in the project, which is a possibility in a more diversified sponsoring corporation because of competition for resources. Moreover, when a PPP is set up as a division within a diversified corporation, the free cash flows produced by the PPP in its operating phase may be diverted away from debt repayment toward higher-yielding (but riskier) uses. Because the SPV has no growth opportunities, the possibility of diverting resources away from creditors is limited. The project's cash flow can therefore be credibly pledged to bondholders, allowing a higher gearing.

It is usually better to select a concessionaire through a competitive auction than with negotiations: it is more transparent, and competition is likely to improve the results. It is also desirable to keep the award conditions simple, to enable firms to evaluate the risks associated with their offer and thus keep them realistic, reducing the possibility of the winner's curse. The auction should also include a vetting process (that is, a request for qualifications), so that only qualified firms are allowed to bid for the project.

An important consideration when designing PPP contracts is the correct assignment of risk. The principle is that the contract should allocate risks to maximize project value, taking into account moral hazard, adverse selection, and risk-bearing capacity. This implies that endogenous risks should be borne by the party best equipped to control them, as this creates incentives to be efficient. Construction, operation, and maintenance

(O&M) risk and performance risk are largely controlled by the concessionaire, who should bear them. Operational risk – keeping the facility well maintained and available – should also be borne by the concessionaire. By contrast, residual value risk (uncertainty about the value of the assets at the end of the PPP contract) and policy risks specific to the project (for example, building a close substitute to the PPP facility), should be borne by the government.

Exogenous risks should be borne by the party best able to diversify them. This is a general statement, but in practice it means that the parties should not bear risks that they do not bear routinely. Consequently, the government should not bear interest or exchange rate risks (and more general, macro risk), which are typically borne by private firms in almost any industry. Similarly, the concessionaire should not bear exogenous demand risk for public infrastructure – taxpayers typically bear this risk.

It follows that PPPs that do not generate user-fee revenues should use availability contracts, so that the firm receives an annual or monthly payment, conditional on the facility meeting well-defined performance standards bearing operational but not demand risk. By contrast, shadow fees should be avoided, as these contracts force the concessionaire to bear demand risk to no useful purpose.

For highways, airports, and other infrastructure facilities it is often the case that user fee revenues will eventually be sufficient to pay for the project, including its operating and maintenance costs. Because of unpredictable demand, though, there may be great uncertainty regarding how long it will take for this to happen. We suggest the use of present-value-of-revenue (PVR) contracts in this case. With this mechanism, the regulator sets the discount rate, the user fee schedule, and an estimate for unitary service costs. Firms bid the present value of user fee revenue they desire, net of service costs. The firm with the lowest bid wins the contract, and the concession ends when the winning firm collects the requested amount of discounted user-fee revenue.

PVR contracts eliminate demand risk, which reduces the risk premium associated with the project relative to the case of fixed-term contracts. PVR contracts also facilitate contract renegotiation without fostering opportunistic renegotiations. This occurs because PVR, by its nature, includes a straightforward estimate for the residual value of the contract to the concessionaire at any point in time, namely the difference between the winning bid and the discounted value of revenues collected at that time net of service costs. This estimate provides fair compensation for the firm if the government chooses early termination of the contract.

Flexible-term PPP contracts have their downside, however. They provide weaker incentives to engage in demand-enhancing investments because the only direct effect is to shorten the term of the franchise. Under a fixed-term franchise, such investments raise demand – and therefore revenue – during the fixed term of the franchise. This suggests that the PVR method is appropriate when service quality can be enforced and when demand is not very responsive to the actions of the concessionaire.

Governance

Governments face three challenges when delivering infrastructure services. First, they have to decide what and when to build. Second, the life-cycle costs of the project should be minimized. Third, governments must ensure that the project receives proper maintenance and service quality. In many countries, traditional public works authorities are entrusted with these three tasks. Not surprisingly, many PPP units, often departments within the public works authority, have simply taken over all these tasks. In this book we have argued that this governance structure is rife with conflicts of interest, because planning, project delivery, regulation, contract supervision, and conflict resolution are entrusted to the same authority.

Our ambitious proposal separates different roles in different institutions, so that conflicts of interest are moderated. The PPP unit should be restricted to project planning, design, and delivery. Before projects are approved, they should be subject to social cost-benefit evaluation by an agency that is independent of the PWA (to ensure consistency with the rest of public investment policy) and then reviewed and approved by the same independent board that reviews traditional infrastructure projects (above a certain size) to ensure a global vision for new infrastructure. An independent PPP superintendency should supervise compliance with the PPP contract and an independent expert panel should review renegotiations and arbitrate conflicts. This proposal addresses the enormous pressures brought to bear on the PPP unit (or more generally on the delivery unit of traditionally procured infrastructure) by setting up checks and balances at the stages of project approval, delivery, and use. A recent wave of reforms of existing PPP legislation in various countries in Latin America has implemented some of these proposals.

Fiscal Accounting

One of the main points of this book is that PPPs are public projects from a fiscal perspective. They increase the deficit and public debt in all but name and affect the intertemporal budget constraint in much the same way as traditional provision. Hence, the accounting treatment of PPPs should be no different from the treatment of standard public investments. Symmetric treatment would make fiscal considerations irrelevant when deciding between a PPP and traditional provision for a given project.

To see what this implies in practice, consider that under the rules of fiscal accounting, traditional provision investment spending increases the current deficit and the stock of public debt. For the same reason, PPP investments should be counted as government spending and added to the stock of government debt. This treatment should extend to additional investments decided in renegotiations. The general rule should be that whenever the concessionaire invests, the current deficit and the stock of public debt should increase one for one with the amount invested.

Under current accounting practices, PPPs affect subsequent budgets when cash disbursements (transfers) are paid to the concessionaire. Our proposal is to compute the implicit yearly debt amortization and include in each year's deficit only the difference between any transfers to the concessionaire and debt amortization.[1] It can be shown that this simple rule replicates, year by year, the outcomes of accounting rules under traditional provision, even when user fees fully pay for the PPP.

9.3 The Future of PPPs

As Klein and Roger (1994) have documented, the current wave of PPPs is only the most recent of many. Spain and France used PPPs to upgrade their roads in the 1960s and 1970s; the United Kingdom and the United States privately funded highways, waterways, railways, and utilities in the nineteenth century; and some authors trace PPPs some 2,000 years back (Bezançon, 2004). Yet the surge in the late nineteenth and early twentieth centuries ended with the nationalization of infrastructure services, in many cases as a response to the inability of private firms to coordinate and deal with network externalities, to underinvestment in response to regulatory takings and to ideological prejudices. In this book we have argued that PPPs can potentially play an important and largely positive role in the execution of infrastructure policy, especially in roads, airports, and ports. But we also believe that to achieve their potential, reforms are needed that ensure successful PPP programs.

---

[1] The obligation with the concessionaire will be fully amortized by the time the concession ends.

To some extent, the current state of affairs is unsurprising. As PPPs spread throughout the world during the past two decades, practice ran ahead of a clear understanding of the economics and politics of PPPs, and governments and private firms took advantage of the opportunities to advance their own interests. More is known today about the types of infrastructure for which PPPs are suitable, about the fiscal rules that should account for them, and about the types of contracts needed to align incentives. Therefore, we can expect progress toward better rules and governance.

The dismissal of Britain's Ryrie Rules, however, suggests that incentives and political self-interest rather than ignorance may be the main reason for the lack of progress in improving PPP contracts, governance, and accounting rules. In several countries, PPPs were a useful trick for governments to increase spending without congressional oversight and the industry that emerged lobbied and pressured governments to create rents to their benefit. The adoption of new procedures and rules is often hampered by the bureaucratic fear that they will be less effective than proven – if imperfect – methods, or by the reaction of industry incumbents to the threat to their rents. The capture of the public works authority by political interests is a major hurdle to reform.

Recent developments in the PPP industry do not suggest that reform is viewed as indispensable. The emerging economies of Brazil, China, and India have been among the main users of PPPs to satisfy their growing demand for infrastructure. The lack of a clear institutional framework in these countries casts doubts on the belief that PPPs will realize their potential. Thus far the fast growth and the need to find outlets for massive savings have counteracted this basic weakness of China's PPP program. Nevertheless, fast growth cannot go on forever, and China's circumstances are not replicable. A fiscal crisis or a major corruption scandal may provide the opportunity to improve PPPs along the lines suggested in this book, or may lead to their demise.

Many observers predicted that the current financial crisis would boost PPPs in Europe and the United States and perhaps induce reform. With severely strained public finances, PPPs might be seen as a means of preventing severe cutbacks in infrastructure spending. Indeed, at the time of writing, several European countries were reconsidering their use of PPPs. According to EIB :

Some countries such as Italy and Slovenia see PPPs as means to foster economic growth. France has also strengthened its efforts to keep its PPP program ongoing and Spain launched an "Extraordinary Infrastructure Plan" this summer, which among others underpins the use of PPPs. The Dutch government announced a boost to infrastructure spending in the next two decades including transport projects procured as PPPs. (EIB, 2011a)

Current events, however, seem less encouraging. With the onset of the crisis PPP finance dried up, as most monolines withdrew from the market. Similarly, banks, the biggest category of private lenders, cut lending as part of their deleveraging. According to EIB (2011b), yearly PPP spending in Europe fell from about €25 billion before the crisis to €18 billion since 2009. More important, equity finance as percentage of the total investment fell and governments and multilaterals like the European Investment Bank stepped in, extending guarantees and even providing credit directly. Moreover, PPP spending has fallen considerably in Britain, no doubt in part as a consequence of the crisis, but also because it has become apparent that perhaps the main stimulus behind the PFI initiative was to sidestep budgetary limits.

So far the experience with PPPs suggests that the trial, error, and correction essential to the democratic process may be tortuous and slow. Clear objectives based on sound economic principles are indispensable if governments are to take advantage of windows of opportunity to introduce the necessary reforms. In any case, it seems that the recommendations summarized in this book will be easier to implement in countries that are just beginning their PPP programs than in countries where the PPP industry is already established. More broadly, it is an open question whether the shortcomings of current PPPs will be addressed and corrected in time or will prove in retrospect to be the cause of the demise of the current PPP wave. That would be a pity. As argued throughout this book, well-designed PPPs can solve the fundamental shortcomings of public infrastructure provision in roads, airports, and ports, produce important efficiency gains due to the incentives they provide for timely maintenance and lower life-cycle costs, and even force the restructuring of public works authorities. These efficiency gains would free resources, not because private financing substitutes for public financing, but because well-designed PPPs provide better quality of service at lower cost.

Appendix

Formal Model

In this appendix we formalize many of the economic arguments used throughout this book using a unified framework.[1] The model we present distinguishes between user fees and government transfers as sources of finance for PPPs. The model also assigns an important role to demand uncertainty.

Result 1 formalizes our claim that preferring PPPs over public provision because PPPs release public resources is wrong. In our benchmark model, the optimal contractual arrangement under public provision is equivalent, from a social welfare perspective, with the optimal PPP contract. Result 2 shows how to implement the optimal infrastructure contract, both under conventional provision and under a PPP. Result 3 shows that, when the benchmark model is extended to incorporate the costs of disbursing public funds, PPPs are better than conventional provision and a PVR auction implements the contract. Results 4 and 5 establish the optimality of PPP contracts over conventional provision when we extend the benchmark model to incorporate moral hazard. These results combine the arguments in favor of PPPs from the "bundling" and "property rights" literatures. A PVR auction also implements the optimal contract. Result 6 shows that in the extension with moral hazard, higher financing costs under PPPs are socially desirable because they provide incentives for innovation.

Result 1 played a central role in Sections 6.1 and 6.2, results 2 and 3 in Sections 2.3 and 6.3, results 4 and 5 in Section 4.2, and result 6 in Section 5.2.

---

[1] Sections 1 through 4 are based on Engel et al. (2013) while Section 5 is based on Engel et al. (2012).

A.1 Basic Setup

A risk-neutral, benevolent social planner desires to select firms to build, operate, and maintain an infrastructure project. The planner must choose between conventional provision, where one firm builds the project and a separate firm maintains and operates it, and a public-private partnership (PPP), where a single firm is in charge of construction, maintenance, and operations. The firm controls the infrastructure assets during the operational phase under a PPP, but not under conventional provision.[2,3]

All firms are identical, risk-averse expected utility maximizers, with preferences represented by the strictly concave utility function u.[4] The technical characteristics of the project are exogenous and many firms can build it at the same cost $I > 0$.

Demand for the project is constant and completely inelastic, and may be high (Q_H), with probability π_H or low (Q_L), with probability π_L, where $\pi_L + \pi_H = 1$ and $Q_H > Q_L > 0$. This probability distribution is common knowledge to firms and the planner. There is a fixed price per unit of service equal to one, constant across demand states.

The upfront investment does not depreciate and service standards are contractible.[5] Maintenance costs are proportional to usage, and without loss of generality we assume that the constant of proportionality is zero.[6]

---

[2] Privatization is ruled out, say, because the project is part of a network, so that long-term government planning is essential, and this is easier if concessions eventually return to the public sector.

[3] This basic setup does not encompass incentive problems, which we incorporate later, in Section PPP.

[4] This should be interpreted as a reduced form for an agency problem that prevents the firm, or more accurately, its controller, from diversifying risk. For a model, see appendix D in the working paper version of Engel et al. (2001). Martimort and Pouyet (2008) also assume a risk-averse concessionaire; see also Dewatripont and Legros (2005) and Hart (2003). Others are skeptical, and point out that private firms can use the capital market to diversify risks at least as well as the government (Hemming, 2006; Klein, 1997). For a discussion of the controversy in economics, see Brealey, Cooper, and Habib (1997). This also underlies the move in some European countries away from shadow toll contracts toward availability payments.

[5] That is, they can be specified and enforced by independent parties at a low cost. Without loss of generality we assume that this cost is zero. See Box 3.1 in the main text for a case study showing that this assumption is appropriate for highways.

[6] Assuming maintenance costs are proportional to demand for the project is a good approximation for many types of infrastructure, including highways and rail lines.

Planner's Problem

Let PS denote producer surplus in state i and CS_i consumer surplus in state i. We assume the planner only considers consumer surplus in the social welfare function.[7,8] The planner's objective is to maximize[9]

$$\sum_{i=H,L} \pi_i CS_i \tag{1}$$

subject to the firm's participation constraint

$$\sum_{i=H,L} \pi_i u(PS_i) \geq u(0) \tag{2}$$

where $u(0)$ is the value the firm assigns to its outside option.

The planner sets the contract length and subsidy in each demand state. Using T_i to denote the contract length and S_i to denote the present value of subsidies it receives in state i, we have:

$$PS_i = PVR_i(T_i) + S_i - I \tag{3}$$

with

$$PVR_i(T_i) \equiv \int_0^{T_i} Q_i e^{-rt} dt = \frac{Q_i(1 - e^{-rT_i})}{r}, \qquad i = H, L; \tag{4}$$

where r is the risk-free interest rate, common across firms and the planner.

By subsidy we mean any cash transfer from the government to the concessionaire. It may be the upfront payment the government makes under conventional provision (in which case S_i is the same for all i; it could also be a cash transfer made over time, contingent on demand, to supplement revenue from the project under a PPP contract, a so-called minimum revenue or minimum income guarantee).

---

[7] This assumption is not essential; see Section 7.

[8] This assumption is justified, for example, when foreign firms are the main investors in PPPs, as is the case in many countries.

[9] This objective function assumes that users' income is uncorrelated with the benefit of using the project, so that if users spend a small fraction of their incomes on project services they will value the benefits produced by the project as if they were risk neutral. See Arrow and Lind (1970). For a criticism, see Baumstark and Gollier (2013).

If the term of the concession is finite in state i ($T_i < \infty$), the government collects user-fee revenue after the concession ends and reduces distortionary taxation elsewhere in the economy. Let $1 + f > 1$ denote the magnitude of this distortion; this expression is often referred to as the *shadow cost of public funds* (see Dahlby, 2008). Then,

$$
\begin{aligned}
CS_i &= [PVR_i^\infty - PVR_i(T_i) - (1 + f)S_i] + f[PVR_i^\infty - PVR_i(T_i)] \\
&= (1 + f)[PVR_i^\infty - PVR_i(T_i) - S_i],
\end{aligned}
\tag{5}
$$

where PVR_i^∞ denotes the present value of user-fee revenue when the contract lasts indefinitely, the largest amount of user fees that can be collected, in present value, in demand state i. We assume that the project can be financed with user fees in all demand states, so that $PVR_L^\infty \geq I$.[10]

Consumer surplus is the sum of net surplus from the use of the road and the benefits the government derives from collecting user fees after the franchise ends. The first term in the expression $PVR_i^\infty - PVR_i(T_i) - (1 + f)S_i$ is the difference between users' willingness to pay in state i and the total amount transferred to the firm, where the cost of the subsidy is increased by the tax distortion required to finance it. Because $PVR_i^\infty - PVR_i(T_i)$ equals the total revenue the government collects after the end of the concession, term $f[PVR_i^\infty - PVR_i(T_i)]$ is the reduction in tax-induced distortions due to this increased revenue.

Substituting equation (5) into (1) and equation (3) into (2) we can rewrite the planner's problem as:

$$
\min_{\{T_H \geq 0, T_L \geq 0, S_H \geq 0, S_L \geq 0\}} \sum_{i=H,L} \pi_i[PVR_i(T_i) + S_i].
\tag{6a}
$$

$$
\text{s.t.} \quad \sum_{i=H,L} \pi_i u(PVR_i(T_i) + S_i - I) \geq u(0),
\tag{6b}
$$

where the terms $(1 + f)$ and $\sum_i PVR_i^\infty$ were dropped from the objective function because they do not depend on the problem's choice variables. It follows that the planner chooses among all contracts that satisfy the concessionaire's participation constraint those that minimize the expected transfer.

---

[10] In Section 6.3 we defined these projects as *high-demand projects*.

A.2 An Irrelevance Result

In this section, we prove that the differential cost of funds induced by distortionary taxes under traditional public provision and a PPP does not provide a rationale to favor PPPs (see Section 6.2). It can be seen, from the planner's problem specified in (6a) and (6b) that the per-dollar cost of paying for the project with user fee revenues or subsidies is the same. Social welfare only depends on *total* transfers to the firm, not on how these transfers are split between subsidies and user fees. This is the fundamental insight of the following result:

Result 1 [Irrelevance of the public-cost-of-funds argument] *Any combination of T_H, T_L, S_H and S_L that satisfies $\mathrm{PVR}_i(T_i) + S_i = I$ for $i = H, L$ solves the planner's problem specified by equations (6a) and (6b). Furthermore, the discounted fiscal surplus in state i equals $\mathrm{PVR}_i^\infty - I$ for all optimal contracts, independent of whether they attain under public provision or a PPP.*

Proof Because the firm is risk averse, it follows (6b) that any feasible contract T_H, T_L, S_H, and S_L satisfies

$$\sum_{i=H,L} \pi_i[\mathrm{PVR}_i(T_i) + S_i - I] \geq 0.$$

It follows that the planner's objective function is bounded from below by I.[11] The proof concludes by noting that this lower bound is attained by any contract that satisfies $\mathrm{PVR}_i(T_i) + S_i = I$ for $i = H, L$ and that any such contract is feasible.

For any of the optimal contracts, the discounted fiscal surplus is:

$$\mathrm{PVR}_i^\infty - \mathrm{PVR}_i(T_i) - S_i = \mathrm{PVR}_i^\infty - I,$$

which does not depend on the combination of user fees and government transfers of the optimal contract under consideration.

What are the economics of this result? As noted in Chapter 6, a common reasoning in favor of private provision of infrastructure is based on the idea that subsidies are an expensive means of financing projects because they are paid with distortionary taxes. Yet the multiplicity of optimal subsidy user fee revenue combinations indicates that distortionary taxation $(1 + f > 1)$ is not sufficient to make PPP provision preferable. One feasible contract is that $T_L = T_H = 0$ and $S_L = S_H = I$. This is the traditional approach

[11] Strictly speaking, we are using Jensen's inequality.

to financing in which the government pays for the project upfront. At the other extreme is a PPP contract financed entirely with user fees, where the firm invests I, collects user-fee revenues equal to I in present value, and receives no subsidies.[12] In addition, there is a continuum of intermediate PPP contracts, in which the government provides partial financing. As discussed in Chapter 6, the standard reasoning overlooks that user fees received by the firm and subsidies are perfect substitutes in the planner's objective function. Similarly, even though the time path of deficits will differ across optimal contracts, the discounted surplus is the same for all of them. Resources saved by the government upfront under a PPP are equal, in present value, to resources foregone during the concession.

A.3 Implementation

Implementing any of the optimal contracts described in 1 is straightforward. For example, under the traditional approach, the firm that builds the project is selected in a competitive auction in which firms bid the amounts they request as compensation, and the firm that maintains the project is chosen in another auction. The firm building the project is usually not the one that will maintain it afterward.

In a competitive setting, the firm whose bid is the lowest builds the project in the first auction. In our setting, the Nash equilibrium bid equals I.[13] In the second auction, because we assume that maintenance costs are zero, this is the winning bid.

The optimal contract can also be implemented using a PPP. Because it will play an important role in the following section, we focus on the PPP contract that requires no government transfers to the concessionaire. In this case $PVR_i(T_i) = I$ and $S_i = 0$ for $i = H, L$. This contract is implemented via a so called present-value-of-revenue (PVR) auction. Firms bid on the present value of user fee revenue they require to finance, build, maintain, and operate the project.[14] Flows are discounted at the risk free rate r. The winner is the

---

[12] Here we use the assumption that $PVR_L^\infty \geq I$, for otherwise the project cannot be financed with user fees in the low-demand state.

[13] If the winning bid is less than I, the winner will have a guaranteed loss; if it is greater than I, losers will regret not having bid slightly below the winning bid. An analogous argument shows that the second auction, to select the firm that will maintain the project, will be won by a firm that offers to charge the maintenance cost, which we assumed is zero.

[14] Present values are calculated net of maintenance costs, which are observed by the planner.

firm that makes the lowest bid and the contract lasts until the firm collects the winning bid, at which point the project reverts to the government.

A straightforward argument shows that Nash equilibrium for the auction yields a winning bid equal I. Furthermore, it follows from $PVR_i(T_i) = I$ that

$$e^{-rT_i} = 1 - \frac{rI}{Q_i}, \qquad i = H, L.$$

so that the contract term is longer in low-demand states. Because competitive auctions reveal the value of I, neither implementation requires the planner to know it.[15] We now have the result mentioned in Section 6.3.

Result 2 [Implementation] *Conventional provision and PPPs implement a contract that achieves the optimum described in Result 1. When implemented with a PVR auction, the contract lasts longer when demand is low.*

A.4 Efficiency Gains: Costs of Disbursing Funds

An advantage of PPPs that are fully or partly funded with user-fee revenue is that they reduce the inefficiencies wrought by subsidy transfers. Subsidies cost more than user fees because rigidities in public spending make it more expensive to transfer a dollar to the concessionaire via subsidies than by using user fees. This may be compounded by inefficiencies or corruption within the public works authority. Therefore, the planner is not indifferent between funding the concessionaire with user fees or subsidies.

To capture this wedge, we assume that, in addition to the distortions associated with collecting taxes, transferring one dollar to the concessionaire costs the government $1 + g$, with $g > 0$. The planner's problem (6a)-(6b) then becomes:

$$\min_{\{T_H \geq 0, T_L \geq 0, S_H \geq 0, S_L \geq 0\}} \sum_{i=H,L} \pi_i [PVR_i(T_i) + (1+g)S_i], \tag{7a}$$

$$\text{s.t.} \quad \sum_{i=H,L} \pi_i u(PVR_i(T_i) + S_i - I) \geq u(0). \tag{7b}$$

---

[15] Neither does the planner need know the distribution of demand. All the planner needs to know in the case of implementation via a PVR auction is that user fees finance the project in all demand states.

Result 3 [Optimality of PVR contracts] *If transferring resources to the firm via subsidies is more expensive than doing so via user fees (that is, when $g > 0$), PPPs lead to higher social welfare than public provision. The unique optimal contract satisfies $PVR_i(T_i) = I$ and $S_i = 0$, for $i = H, L$, and can be implemented with a PVR auction.*

Proof The proof is analogous to that of Result 1. In this case, though, the only contract that attains the lower bound of the objective function is the contract with $PVR_L(T_L) = PVR_H(T_H) = I$ and $S_L = S_H = 0$.

A.5 Efficiency Gains: Noncontractible Innovations

As discussed in Chapter 4, when service quality is contractible, bundling of construction and operations provides an argument in favor of PPPs. A closely related argument in favor of PPPs is that firms have stronger incentives to use infrastructure assets more efficiently because they own these assets during the life of the contract, whereas any innovation under conventional provision must be negotiated with the regulator who can appropriate part of the benefits.[16]

This suggests that PPPs can mitigate moral hazard better than public provision. We formalize this insight next.[17] We extend the basic model to incorporate moral hazard and, for simplicity, assume $g = 0$ so that there is no additional cost when transferring subsidies. The model is a simplified version of Engel, Fischer, and Galetovic (2012) and similar to Hart (2003).

During the construction phase, the firm can exert effort $e \geq 0$, at a monetary cost of ke, with $k > 0$. Utility in discounted income and effort, $U(y,e)$, is separable: $U(y,e) = u(y) - ke$. Effort produces an innovation that saves M during the life of the contract with probability $p(e)$, while no savings occur with probability $1 - p(e)$. The probability of success function, $p(e)$, satisfies $p(0) = 0$, $p' > 0$, $p(e) < 1$ and $p'' < 0$.

It is usually difficult for the regulator to monitor the firm's innovation effort. It may also be difficult to write contracts that anticipate the many forms in which the firm's activities may succeed in reducing the cost of operating and maintaining the infrastructure. For these reasons we assume that it is possible to contract neither effort nor innovation.

---

[16] See Hart, Shleifer, and Vishny (1997).

[17] Papers that study this issue are Grout (1997), Hart (2003), Bennett and Iossa (2006a), Bentz, Grout, and Halonen (2005), Martimort and Pouyet (2008), and Iossa and Martimort (2008).

Public Provision

Under public provision, the firm that builds the project is chosen in a competitive auction similar to the one considered in Section 3. Because the benefits from innovation are realized after the building phase, the firm does not invest in effort. It follows that the planner's problem is the one considered in Section 2 with the additional constraint that the firm can only be remunerated with government transfers.

Result 4 [Noncontractible innovations and public provision] *Under public provision, the winning firm bids* I, *exerts no effort, and builds the project at cost* I.

PPP

User fees and government transfers are perfect substitutes in this extension of our benchmark model, which means that we can assume that only user fees are used to remunerate the concessionaire. Then the planner's decision variables are the contract's length in both demand states or, equivalently, the firm's discounted revenues in both demand states. We denote the latter by R_i, $i = H, L$. We have:

$$0 \leq R_i \leq \mathrm{PVR}_i^\infty.$$

The planner's problem is:

$$\min_{\{R_H, R_L, e\}} \sum_{i=H,L} \pi_i R_i \tag{8a}$$

$$\text{s.t. } p(e) \sum_{i=H,L} \pi_i u_i (R_i + M - I) + (1 - p(e)) \sum_{i=H,L} \pi_i u_i (R_i - I) \geq u(0) + ke \tag{8b}$$

$$e = \mathrm{argmax}_{e' \geq 0} \left\{ p(e') \sum_{i=H,L} \pi_i u_i (R_i + M - I) + (1 - p(e')) \sum_{i=H,L} \pi_i u_i (R_i - I) - u(0) - ke' \right\} \tag{8c}$$

$$0 \leq R_i \leq \mathrm{PVR}_i^\infty, \ i = H, L \tag{8d}$$

$$e \geq 0 \tag{8e}$$

The planner's objective (8a) is analogous to the case without moral hazard. Condition (8b) is the firm's participation constraint with moral hazard.

(8c) is the firm's incentive compatibility constraint: once the planner announces a contract (R_H, R_L), the firm will choose effort optimally. The remaining constraints have straightforward interpretations.

Setting up the Lagrangian for the planner's problem (8a)-(8e), the first-order condition implies that $R_H = R_L$ if the solutions are interior, which, we show later, is the case. The planner's problem can therefore be written as:

$$\min_{\{R,e\}} R, \tag{9(a)}$$

$$\text{s.t.} \; p(e)u(R + M - I) + (1 - p(e))u(R - I) \geq u(0) + ke, \tag{9(b)}$$

$$e = \operatorname*{argmax}_{e' \geq 0}\{p(e')u(R + M - I) + (1 - p(e'))u(R - I) - u(0) - ke'\}, \tag{9(c)}$$

$$0 \leq R \leq \mathrm{PVR}_L^\infty, \tag{9(d)}$$

$$e \geq 0. \tag{9(e)}$$

Conditions for Positive Effort

We first consider a contract such that the planner sets $R_i \equiv R = I$, $i = H, L$. This contract is feasible because by assumption we have $\mathrm{PVR}_L^\infty \geq I$. It follows that the firm will choose effort to solve:

$$\max_{e \geq 0} G(e) \equiv \max_{e \geq 0} p(e)u(M) + (1 - p(e))u(0) - ke.$$

Optimal effort will be positive if $G'(0) > 0$, that is, if

$$p'(0)[u(M) - u(0)] > k. \tag{10}$$

Under this condition, the firm is better off than exerting no effort, so its discounted profit is strictly positive because with probability $p(e) > 0$ the firm obtains a return $R + M - I > 0$ when $R = I$.

The interpretation is straightforward. The concessionaire exerts effort if the increase in the probability of succeeding (captured by $p'(0)$) is large, if the benefit from succeeding, $u(M) - u(0)$, is large, or if the cost of effort, k, is small.

We show next that (10) ensures that incentive-compatible levels of effort as a function of R, defined via (9c), are positive and strictly decreasing in R.

Lemma 1 (Effort increases as revenue decreases) *Define $e(R)$ as the solution to (9c). Then, for $R \leq I$ we have that $e > 0$ and $e'(R) < 0$.*

Proof Concavity of u implies that $u(R + M - I) - u(R - I)$ is decreasing in R, which combined with (10) implies that

$$p'(0)[u(R + M - I) - u(R - I)] > k.$$

It follows that $e(R) > 0$ for $R \leq I$. The first-order condition that determines $e(R)$ then is

$$p'(e(R))[u(R + M - I) - u(R - I)] = k. \tag{11}$$

Implicit differentiation of this expression w.r.t. R leads to:

$$e'(R) = -\frac{p'(e)[u'(R + M - I) - u'(R - I)]}{p''(e)[u(R + M - I) - u(R - I)]} < 0$$

As revenue decreases, the incentives to exert effort become stronger because the marginal benefit from exerting effort is larger. The value of an extra dollar is higher when income is low.

Optimal Contract and Implementation

From (9a)-(9e) it follows that the planner's problem is to find the lowest discounted revenue, R^*, for which the firm's participation constraint is satisfied. The following result characterizes R^*.

Result 5 [Optimal contract with moral hazard] *Define $\Pi(R)$ as the concessionaire's expected profit if $R_H = R_L = R$ and the firm chooses $e = e(R)$ defined in Lemma 1. Then (a) $\Pi(R)$ is strictly increasing; (b) the optimal R satisfies $\Pi(R^*) = 0$; (c) $I - M < R^* < I$, so that a PPP is better than public provision and (d) the optimal contract can be implemented with a PVR auction.*

Proof Using the first-order condition (11) we have:

$$\Pi'(R) = p(e)u'(R + M - I) + (1 - p(e))u'(R - I) > 0.$$

It follows that $\Pi(R)$ is strictly increasing. Furthermore, it also follows that the smallest value of R satisfying the firm's participation constraint is the unique solution for $\Pi(R^*) = 0$. As we saw earlier, $\Pi(R = I) > 0$. It is easy to see that $\Pi(R = I - M) < 0$. Thus, $I - M < R^* < I$. Finally, because $\Pi(R)$

is increasing, the straightforward argument used earlier in this appendix shows that a PVR auction implements the optimal contract.

PPP Premium and Noncontractible Innovations

Result 4 showed that under public provision firms exert no effort and bear no risk. The cost of financing debt will therefore be the risk-free discount rate, r. By contrast, when the infrastructure is provided via a PPP the firm exerts effort and bears risk. It follows that the interest rate will be larger than r.

Defining the risk-adjusted discount rate, r^*, as the rate for which the firm's expected discounted profits are equal to zero when the firm's participation constraint is satisfied with equality, a tedious but straightforward calculation (see Engel and Galetovic, 2012, p. 29), shows that:

$$r^* \approx r + \sqrt{\frac{A \times p(e^*)(1 - p(e^*))}{2}} \times \frac{M}{I}.$$

Where $e^* > 0$ denotes the concessionaire's optimal effort and A the concessionaire's coefficient of relative risk aversion, evaluated at expected discounted profits.

While borrowing costs under a PPP are higher than under public provision, it does not mean that providing the infrastructure is more costly under a PPP. The risk the firm bears induces it to exert effort that reduces the user fees and government transfers needed to satisfy the firm's participation constraint from I to $R^* < I$ (see results 4 and 5). Even though *per-dollar* borrowing costs are higher under a PPP, total cost R^* to society is lower.

Result 6 [PPP premiums and high powered contracts] *Under the assumptions of results 4 and 5, the optimal PPP contract leads to higher per-dollar borrowing costs, that is, a PPP premium. Nevertheless, a PPP contract also yields higher welfare because it provides incentives to innovate that reduce user fees and transfers needed to build the infrastructure.*

We conclude that a contractual form that minimizes borrowing costs for the concessionaire may not be desirable. Risk bearing, and the resulting borrowing costs, may mitigate moral hazard, inducing the concessionaire to exert effort that yields higher welfare.

A.6 Relaxing Assumptions

Demand

Assuming two demand states is not essential, nor that demand uncertainty is resolved at $t = 0$. Engel et al. (2013) present versions of results 1, 2 and 3 with a general probability density describing users' discounted willingness to pay. This paper also extends these results to the more general case of standard, price-responsive demand.

The assumption that the upfront investment can be financed in all demand states is dropped in Engel et al. (2013). This paper shows that, in the general case, the optimal contract that extends Result 3 exhibits a minimum income guarantee and an upper bound on the concessionaire's revenues, both in discounted terms. The contract lasts indefinitely in demand states where the concessionaire receives government subsidies. This contract can be implemented via a two-threshold auction, an extension of a PVR auction.

Planner's Objective Function
We assumed that the planner's objective function is to maximize discounted consumer surplus, thereby ignoring producer surplus. In Engel et al. (2013) we consider the general case where the planner's objective function is a weighted average of discounted consumer and producer surplus, with the weight of consumer surplus being larger than or equal to the weight of producer surplus. This includes the conventional case where the planner maximizes total surplus. Results 1, 2 and 3 extend to this case without any modification.

Benefit from Innovation
In Section 5, we assumed that the firm's savings when its efforts succeed do not depend on the length of the concession contract. In Engel et al. (2012) we consider the more realistic case where these benefits increase with the length of the concession contract. With the additional assumption that the concessionaire's coefficient of relative risk aversion A, satisfies $A > M / (1 + M)$, an argument analogous to the one provided in Section 5 proves results 4, 5, and 6.

References

Akintoye, A., M. Beck, and C. Hardcastle, 2003. *Public-Private Partnerships: Managing Risks and Opportunities*. Oxford: Blackwell.

Albalate, D. and G. Bel, 2009. "Regulating Concessions of Toll Motorways: An Empirical Study on Fixed vs. Variable Term Contracts." *Transportation Research Part A: Policy and Practice* 43, 219–229.

Andres, L. and J. L. Guasch, 2008. "Negotiating and Renegotiating PPPs and Concessions," in G. Schwartz, A. Carbacho, and K. Funke (eds.), *Public Investment and Public-Private Partnerships*. Houndmills: Palgrave Macmillan.

Andres L., J. L. Guasch, and S. Straub, 2007. "Do Regulation and Institutional Design Matter for Infrastructure Sector Performance?" Policy Research Working Paper Nr. 4378. Washington, DC: The World Bank.

Arrow, K. and R. Lind, 1970. "Uncertainty and Public Investment Decisions." *American Economic Review* 60, 364–378.

Athias, L. and A. Nuñez, 2008. "Winner's Curse in Toll Road Concessions." *Economic Letters* 101, 172–174.

2009. "The More the Merrier? Number of Bidders, Information Dispersion, Renegotiation and Winner's Curse in Toll Road Concessions." Working Paper 2009/7. Paris: Chaire EPPP.

Athias, L. and S. Saussier, 2010. "Contractual Flexibility or Rigidity for Public Private Partnerships? Theory and Evidence from Infrastructure Concession Contracts." Working Paper 2010/3. Paris: Chaire EPPP.

Auriol, E. and P. Picard, 2013. "A Theory of BOT Concession Contracts." *Journal of Economic Behavior and Organization* 89, 187–209.

Baumstark, L. and C. Gollier, 2013. "The Relevance and the Limits of the Arrow-Lind Theorem." mimeo, IDEI.

Bennett, J. and E. Iossa, 2006a. "Building and Managing Facilities for Public Services." *Journal of Public Economics* 90, 2143–2160.

2006b. "Delegation of Contracting in the Private Provision of Public Services." *Review of Industrial Organization* 29, 75–92.

Bentz, A., P. A. Grout, and M. Halonen, 2005. "What Should Governments Buy from the Private Sector – Assets or Services?" mimeo, University of Bristol.

Besley, T. and M. Ghatak, 2001. "Government versus Private Ownership of Public Goods." *Quarterly Journal of Economics* 116, 1343–1370.

de Bettignies, J. and T. W. Ross, 2004. "The Economics of Public-Private Partnerships." *Canadian Public Policy* 30, 135–154.

2009. "Public-Private Partnerships and the Privatization of Financing: An Incomplete Contracts Approach." *International Journal of Industrial Organization* 27, 358–368.

Bezançon, X., 2004. *2000 ans d'histoire du partenariat public-privé*. Paris: Presses de l' Ecole Nationale Des Ponts et Chausses.

Bitrán, E., 2011. "Alianzas público-privadas en América Latina: hacia una mayor eficiencia y desarrollo institucional." *Slide presentation*. Santiago: Universidad Adolfo Ibáñez.

Bitrán, E. and M. Villena, 2010. "El nuevo desafío de las concesiones de obras públicas en Chile: hacia una mayor eficiencia y desarrollo institucional." *Estudios Públicos* 117, 175–217.

Bitsch, F., A. Buchner, and C. Kaserer, 2010. "Risk, Return and Cash Flow Characteristics of Infrastructure Fund Investments." *EIB Papers* 15, 106–136.

Blanc-Brude, F., H. Goldsmith, and T. Välilä, 2007. "Public-Private Partnerships in Europe: An Update." Economic and Financial Report Nr. 2007/03. Luxembourg: European Investment Bank.

Blanchard, O. and F. Giavazzi, 2004. "Improving the SGP through a Proper Accounting of Public Investment." Discussion Paper Nr. 4220. London: CEPR.

Brainard, W. and F. T. Dolbear, 1971. "Social Risk and Financial Markets." *American Economic Review* 61, 361–370.

Brealey, R. A., I. A. Cooper, and M. A. Habib, 1997. "Investment Appraisal in the Public Sector." *Oxford Review of Economic Policy* 13, 12–27.

Broadbent, J., and R. Laughlin, 2005. "Government Concerns and Tensions in Accounting Standard Setting: The Case of Accounting for the Private Finance Initiative in the U.K." *Accounting and Business Research* 35, 207–228.

Broadbent, J. and R. Laughlin, 2008. "Identifying and Controlling Risk: The Problems of Uncertainty in the Private Finance Initiative in the U.K.'s National Health Service." *Critical Perspectives on Accounting* 19, 40–78.

de Brux, J., 2010. "The Dark and Bright Side of Renegotiation: An Application to Transport Concession Contracts." *Utilities Policy* 18, 77–85.

Buiter, W. and S. Fries, 2002. "What Should the Multilateral Development Banks Do?" Working Paper Nr. 74. London: European Bank for Reconstruction and Development.

Cadot, O., L. H. Röller, and A. Stephan, 2006. "Contribution to Productivity or Pork Barrel? The Two Faces of Infrastructure Investment." *Journal of Public Economics* 90, 1133–1153.

Cangiano, M., R. Hemming, and T. Ter-Minassian, 2004. "Public-Private Partnerships: Implications for Public Finances," in F. Balassone, D. Franco, and S Zotteri (eds.), *Public Debt*. Rome: Banca D'Italia.

Capen, E. C., R.t V. Clapp, and W. M. Campbell, 1971. "Competitive Bidding in High-Risk Situations." *Journal of Petroleum Technology* 23, 641–653.

Chadwick, E., 1859. "Results of Different Principles of Legislation in Europe." *Journal of the Royal Statistical Society* A22, 381–420.

Chen, A. and K. Subprasom, 2007. "Analysis of Regulation and Policy of Private Toll Roads in a Build-Operate-Transfer Scheme under Demand Uncertainty." *Transportation Research Part A: Policy and Practice* 41, 537–558.

Cheng, C. and Z. Wang, 2009. "Public-Private Partnerships in China: Making Progress in a Weak Governance Environment." Briefing Series Nr. 56. Nottingham: The University of Nottingham China Policy Institute.

Cheng, J., 2010. "The Chicago Skyway Concession." Senior thesis. New Haven, CT: Yale University.

Chong, E., F. Huet, and S. Saussier, 2006. "Auctions, Ex Post Competition and Prices: The Efficiency of Public-Private Partnerships." *Annals of Public and Cooperative Economics* 77, 517–549.

Congressional Budget Office, 2008. *Issues and Options in Infrastructure Investment.* Washington, DC: Congressional Budget Office.

Connolly, C., G. Martin, and A. Wall, 2008. "Education, Education, Education: The Third Way and PFI." *Public Administration* 86, 951–968.

Dahlby, B., 2008. *The Marginal Cost of Public Funds: Theory and Applications.* Cambridge, MA: MIT Press.

Daniels, R. and M. Trebilcock, 1996. "Private Provision of Public Infrastructure: An Organizational Analysis of the Next Privatization Frontier." *University of Toronto Law Journal* 46, 375–426.

2000. "An Organizational Analysis of the Public-Private Partnership in the Provision of Public Infrastructure," in P. Vaillancourt-Roseneau (ed.), *Public-Private Policy Partnerships.* Cambridge, MA: MIT Press.

Defossé, J. C., 1990. *Le Petit Guide des Grands Travaux Inutiles.* Brussels: Paul Legrain & RTBF Édition.

Demsetz, H. 1968. "Why Regulate Utilities?" *Journal of Law and Economics* 11, 55–66.

Dewatripont, M. and P. Legros, 2005. "Public-Private Partnerships: Contract Design and Risk Transfer." *EIB Papers* 10, 120–145.

Domberger, S. and P. Jensen, 1997. "Contracting Out by the Public Sector: Theory, Evidence, Prospects." *Oxford Review of Economic Policy* 13, 67–78.

Donaghue, B., 2002. "Statistical Treatment of Build-Operate-and-Transfer Schemes." Working Paper Nr. 02/167, Washington, DC: International Monetary Fund.

Donahue, J. D. and R. Zeckhauser, 2011.*Collaborative Governance: Private Roles for Public Goals in Turbulent Times.* Princeton, NJ: Princeton University Press.

Dos Santos-Senna, L. A. and F. Dutra-Michel, 2008. *Rodovias autosustentadas.* São Paulo: Editora CLA Cultural.

Economic Planning Advisory Commission, 1995. *Final Report of the Private Infrastructure Task Force.* Canberra: Australian Government Publishing Service.

Economist Intelligence Unit, 2009. "Partnerships for Progress? Evaluating the Environment for Public-Private Partnerships in Latin America and the Caribbean." Washington, DC: Inter-American Development Bank.

Engel, E., R. Fischer, and A. Galetovic, 1996. "Licitación de carreteras en Chile." *Estudios Públicos* 61, 5–38.

1997a. "Infrastructure Franchising and Government Guarantees," in T. Irwin, M. Klein, G. Perry, and M. Thobani (eds.), *Dealing with Public Risk in Private Infrastructure.* Washington, DC: The World Bank.

1997b. "Respuesta a Michael Klein y Jean Tirole." *Estudios Públicos* 67, 215–225.

2001. "Least-Present-Value-of-Revenue Auctions and Highway Franchising." *Journal of Political Economy* 109, 993–1020.

2003. "Privatizing Highways in Latin America: Fixing What Went Wrong." *Economia, the Journal of Lacea* 4, 129–158.

2004. "How to Auction an Essential Facility When Underhand Agreements Are Possible." *Journal of Industrial Economics* 52, 427–455.

2008. "*Renegotiation and Corruption.*" mimeo, Yale University.

2009. "Soft Budgets and Renegotiations in Public-Private Partnerships." Working Paper Nr. 15300. Cambridge: NBER.

2011. "Public-Private Partnerships to Revamp U.S. Infrastructure." Discussion paper 2011–02. Washington, DC: The Hamilton Project – Brookings Institution.

2012. "Is There a PPP Interest Rate Premium?" mimeo, Yale University, Department of Economics.

2013. "The Basic Public Finance of Public-Private Partnerships." *Journal of the European Economic Association* 11, 83–111.

Engel, E., R. Fischer, A. Galetovic, and M. Hermosilla, 2009. "Renegociación de concesiones en Chile." *Estudios Públicos* 113, 151–205.

Engel, E. and A. Galetovic, 2012. "Social Evaluation of Infrastructure Projects: When Public? When PPP? When at All?" mimeo, Universidad de los Andes.

Estache, A., 2006. "PPI Partnerships vs. PPI Divorces in LDCs." *Review of Industrial Organization* 29, 3–26.

Estache, A., J. L. Guasch, A. Iimi, and L. Trujillo, 2009. "Multidimensionality and Renegotiation: Evidence from Transport-Sector Public-Private-Partnership Transactions in Latin America." *Review of Industrial Organization* 35, 41–71.

Eurostat. 2004. "Treatment of Public-Private Partnerships." Press release (February). Luxembourg: Eurostat.

Eurostat, 2010. *Manual on Government Deficit and Debt – Implementation of ESA 95 – 2010 edition.* Luxembourg: Publications Office of the European Union.

Federal Highway Administration (FHWA), 1999. "Conditions & Performance." Washington, DC: U.S. Department of Transportation.

2010. "Conditions & Performance." Washington, DC: U.S. Department of Transportation.

2011. *Deficient Bridges by State and Highway System.* Washington, DC: U.S. Department of Transportation.

Fitch Ratings, 2010. "Rating Criteria for Availability-Based Infrastructure Projects." Technical Report. London and New York: Fitch Ratings.

Flyvbjerg, B., M. Holm, and S. Buhl, 2002. "Underestimating Costs in Public Works Projects: Error or Lie?" *Journal of the American Planning Association* 68, 279–295.

2005. "How (In)accurate Are Demand Forecasts in Public Works Projects?: The Case of Transportation." *Journal of the American Planning Association* 71, 131–146.

Gerrard, M., 2001. "Public-Private Partnerships." *Finance and Development* 38, 48–51.

Gómez-Ibañez, J. A. and J. Meyer, 1993. *Going Private: The International Experience with Transport Privatization.* Washington, DC: Brookings Institution.

Grimsey, D. and M. K. Lewis, 2002. "Evaluating the Risks of Public-Private Partnerships for Infrastructure Projects," *International Journal of Project Management* 20, 107–118.

2004a. *The Economics of Public-Private Partnerships.* Northampton: Edward Elgar.

2004b. "The Governance of Contractual Relationships in Public Private Partnerships," *Journal of Corporate Citizenship* 15, 91–109.

2005a. "Are Public Private Partnerships Value for Money? Evaluating Alternative Approaches and Comparing Academic and Practitioner Views." *Accounting Forum* 29, 345–378.

2005b. *Public-Private Partnerships*. Northampton: Edward Elgar.

2007. "Public Private Partnerships and Public Procurement." *Agenda* 14, 171–188.

Grout, P. A., 1997. "The Economics of the Private Finance Initiative." *Oxford Review of Economic Policy* 13, 53–66.

2003. "Public and Private Sector Discount Rates in Public-Private Partnerships." *Economic Journal* 113, C62–C68.

2005. "Value-for-Money Measurement in Public-Private Partnerships." *EIB Economic Studies* 10, 32–56.

Grout, P. A. and S. Sonderegger, 2006. "Simple Money-Based Tests for Choosing Between Private and Public Delivery: A Discussion of the Issues." *Review of Industrial Organization* 29, 93–126.

Grout, P. A. and M. Stevens, 2003. "Financing and Managing Public Services–An Assessment." *Oxford Review of Economic Policy* 19, 215–234.

Guasch, J. L., 2004. *Granting and Renegotiating Infrastructure Concessions: Doing It Right*. Washington, DC: The World Bank.

Guasch, J. L., J. J. Laffont, and S. Straub, 2006. "Renegotiation of Concession Contracts: A Theoretical Approach." *Review of Industrial Organization* 29, 55–73.

2007. "Concessions of Infrastructure in Latin America: Government-led Renegotiation." *Journal of Applied Econometrics* 22, 1267–1294.

2008. "Renegotiation of Concession Contracts in Latin America: Evidence from the Water and Transport Sectors." *International Journal of Industrial Organization* 26, 421–442.

Guasch, J. L. and S. Straub, 2006. "Renegotiation of Infrastructure Concessions: An Overview." *Annals of Public and Cooperative Economics* 77, 479–493.

2009. "Corruption and Concession Renegotiations: Evidence from the Water and Transport Sectors in Latin America." *Utilities Policy* 17, 185–190.

Hall, J., 1998. "Private Opportunity, Public Benefit?" *Fiscal Studies* 19, 121–140.

Harrison, D., 2007. *History of U.K. PPPs*. London: Partnerships U.K.

Harstad, R. and M. Crew, 1999. "Franchise Bidding without Holdups: Utility Regulation with Efficient Pricing and Choice of Provider." *Journal of Regulatory Economics* 15, 141–163.

Hart, O., 2003. "Incomplete Contracts and Public Ownership: Remarks and an Application to Public-Private Partnerships." *Economic Journal* 113, C69–C76.

Hart, O., A. Shleifer, and R. Vishny, 1997. "The Proper Scope of Government: Theory and an Application to Prisons." *Quarterly Journal of Economics* 112, 1127–1161.

Heald, D., 1997. "Privately Financed Capital in Public Services." *The Manchester School* 65, 568–598.

2010. "The Accounting Treatment of Private Finance Initiative Projects," in *Pre-Budget Report 2009*. London: House of Commons.

Heald, D. and G. Georgiou . 2011. "The Substance of Accounting for Public-Private Partnerships." *Financial Accountability & Management* 27, 17–247.

Heald, D. and A. McLeod, 2002. "Public Expenditure," in *Constitutional Law, 2002, The Laws of Scotland: Stair Memorial Encyclopaedia*. Edinburgh: Butterworths.

Heggie, I. G. and P. Vickers, 1998. "Commercial Management and Financing of Roads." Technical Paper Nr. 409. Washington, DC: The World Bank.

Hellowell, M., 2007. *Evidence to the National Assembly for Wales Finance Committee with Regard to Its Inquiry on Public Private Partnerships.* University of Edinburgh: School of Social and Political Science.

Hemming, R., 2004. "Public Private Partnerships." Technical report. Washington, DC: International Monetary Fund.

2006. *Public-Private Partnerships, Government Guarantees and Fiscal Risk.* Washington, DC: International Monetary Fund.

2008. "Some Accounting and Reporting Issues," in G. Schwartz, A. Carbacho, and K. Funke (eds.), *Public Investment and Public-Private Partnerships.* Houndmills: Palgrave Macmillan.

Hirshleifer, J., 1966. "Investment Decision under Uncertainty: Application of the State-Preference Approach." *Quarterly Journal of Economics* 80, 252–277.

Hodges, J. T. and G. Dellacha, 2007. "Unsolicited Infrastructure Proposals: How Some Countries Introduce Competition and Transparency." Working paper Nr. 1. Washington, DC: PPIAF.

H. M. Treasury, 1999. "How to Construct a Public Sector Comparator." Technical Note Nr. 5 London: Treasury Taskforce.

2003. *PFI: Meeting the Investment Challenge.* London: H. M. Treasury.

2008a. "Making Changes in Operational PFI Projects." Thirty-sixth Report of Session 2007–08. London: H. M. Treasury.

2008b. *Infrastructure Procurement: Delivering Long-Term Value.* London: H. M. Treasury.

2011. "UK Private Finance Initiative Projects: Summary Data." London: H. M. Treasury.

Ho, P., 2006. "The Development of Public-Private Partnerships in China." *Surveyors Times* 15, 1–12.

House of Lords Select Committee on Economic Affairs. 2010. *Private Finance Projects and Off-Balance Sheet Debt.* Volume 1: Report, First Report of Session 2009–10. Richmond: H. M. Stationery Office.

International Monetary Fund (IMF). 2004. "Public-Private Partnerships." mimeo, Washington, DC: IMF.

Inderst, G., 2010. "Infrastructure as an Asset Class." *EIB Papers* 15, 70–104.

Iossa, E. and D. Martimort, 2008. "The Simple Microeconomics of Public-Private Partnerships." Mimeo, University of Toulouse.

2012. "Risk Allocation and the Cost and Benefits of Public-Private Partnerships." *RAND Journal of Economics* 43, 442–474.

Irwin, T., 2007. *Government Guarantees: Allocating and Valuing Risk in Privately Financed Infrastructure Projects.* Washington, DC: The World Bank.

Iseki, H., J. Eckert, K. Uchida, R. Dunn, and B. D. Taylor, 2009. "Task B-2: Status of Legislative Settings to Facilitate Public-Private Partnerships in the U.S." Research Report Nr. 32. Berkeley: University of California, Institute of Transportation Studies.

Jenkinson, T., 2003. "Private Finance." *Oxford Review of Economic Policy* 19, 323–334.

Jensen, P. and R. Stonecash, 2005. "Incentives and the Efficiency of Public Sector-Outsourcing Contracts." *Journal of Economic Surveys* 19, 766–787.

de Jong, M., M. Rui, D. Stead, M. Yongchi, and X. Bao, 2010. "Introducing Public-Private Partnerships for Metropolitan Subways in China: What is the Evidence?" *Journal of Transport Geography* 18, 301–313.

Kappeler A. and M Nemoz, 2010. "Public-Private Partnerships in Europe – Before and during the Recent Financial Crisis," *Economic and Financial Report 2010/04, European Investment Bank.*

Kay, J., 1993. "Efficiency and Private Capital in the Provision of Infrastructure," in *Infrastructure Policies for the 1990s.* Paris: OECD.

Ke, Y., S. Wang, and A. P. C. Chan, 2009. "Public-Private Partnerships in China's Infrastructure Development: Lessons Learnt," in H. Wamelink, M. Prins, and R. Geraedlts (eds.), *Proceedings of the International Conference on Changing Roles: New Roles and New Challenges.* Tilburg: Tilburg University.

Ke, Y., S. Wang, A. P. C. Chan, and P. T. I. Lam, 2010. "Preferred Risk Allocation in China's Public-Private Partnership (PPP) Projects." *International Journal of Project Management* 28, 482–492.

Khadaroo, I., 2008. "The Actual Evaluation of School PFI Bids for Value for Money in the U.K. Public Sector." *Critical Perspectives on Accounting* 19, 1321–1345.

King, S. and R. Pitchford. 2008. "Private or Public? Towards a Taxonomy of Optimal Ownership and Management Regimes." *Economic Record* 84, 366–377.

Klein, D. B. and J. Majewski, 2008. "Turnpikes and Toll Roads in Nineteenth Century America," in R. Whaples (ed.), *EH.Net Encyclopedia.*

Klein, M., 1997. "The Risk Premium for Evaluating Public Projects." *Oxford Review of Economic Policy* 13, 29–42.

Klein, M. and N. Roger, 1994. "Back to the Future: The Potential in Infrastructure Privatization," in R. O'Brian (ed.), *Finance and the International Economy.* Oxford: Oxford University Press.

KPMG. 2009. *Infrastructure in China: Foundation for Growth.* Hong Kong: KPMG.

Laffont, J. J. and J. Tirole, 1993. *A Theory of Incentives in Procurement and Regulation.* Cambridge, MA: MIT Press.

Levy, S. M. 1996. *Build, Operate, Transfer: Paving the Road for Tomorrow's Infrastructure.* New York: John Wiley & Sons.

Lomax, T., D. Schrank, and S. Turner, 2010. *Urban Mobility Report 2010.*Riverside: Texas Transportation Institute.

Martimort, D. and J. Pouyet, 2008. "To Build or Not to Build: Normative and Positive Theories of Private-Public Partnerships." *International Journal of Industrial Organization* 26, 392–411.

Maskin, E. and J. Tirole, 2008. "Public-Private Partnerships and Government Spending Limits." *International Journal of Industrial Organization* 26, 412–420.

National Accounting Office (NAO), 2009. *Performance of PFI Construction.* London: NAO.

2011. *Lessons from PFI and Other Projects.* London: NAO.

Nombela, G. and G. de Rus . 2004. "Flexible-Term Contracts for Road Franchising." *Transportation Research Part A* 38, 163–179.

Nossaman LLP, 2011. "Overview of States with Significant Transportation Public Private Partnership Authority," in http://www.nossaman.com.

OECD, 2008. *Public-Private Partnerships: In Pursuit of Risk Sharing and Value for Money.* Paris: OECD.

Office of Government Commerce, 2002. *Best Practice: Value for Money Evaluation in Complex Procurement.* London: OGC.

Poole, R. J., 2006. "Lessons Learned from Early PPP Toll Road Projects." Presentation to the Florida Transportation Commission.

Portugal, M., 2010. *Concessões e PPPs: melhores práticas em licitações e contratos.* mimeo.

Posner, R. 1972. "The Appropriate Scope of Regulation in Cable Television." *Bell Journal of Economics* 3, 335–358.

Price Waterhouse Coopers, 2008. *The Value of PFI: Hanging in the Balance (Sheet)?* London: Price Waterhouse Coopers.

Quispe, E. and S. Cartier, 2003. "Microenterprise-Based Road Maintenance in Peru." *ASIST Bulletin* 15, 15–16.

Rall, J., J. B. Reed, and N. J. Farber, 2010. *Public-Private Partnerships for Transportation: A Toolkit for Legislators.* Denver, CO: National Conference of State Legislatures.

de Reugemont, P., 2008. "Accounting for PPPs: The Eurostat Approach," in G. Schwartz, A. Carbacho, and K. Funke (eds.), *Public Investment and Public-Private Partnerships.* Houndmills: Palgrave Macmillan.

Riess, A., 2005. "Is the PPP model Applicable across Sectors?" *EIB Economic Studies* 10, 10–30.

Rioja, Felix K. 2003. "Filling Potholes: Macroeconomic Effects of Maintenance versus New Investments in Public Infrastructure." *Journal of Public Economics* 87, 2281–2304.

Riordan, M. and D. Sappington, 1987. "Awarding Monopoly Franchises." *American Economic Review* 77, 375–387.

Rui, M., 2008. "Public-Private Partnership and the Management of Expressways in China: An Agency Theory Approach." Thesis. Delft: Faculty of Technology, Policy and Management, Delft University of Technology.

Rui, M., M. de Jong, and E. ten Heuvelhof, 2008. "Public-Private Partnerships for Expressways in China: An Agency Theory Approach." Paper presented in the First International Conference on Infrastructure Systems and Services: Building Networks for a Brighter Future (INFRA).

2010. "A Typology of Strategic Behavior in PPPs for Expressways: Lessons from China and Implications for Europe." *European Journal of Transport and Infrastructure Research* 10, 42–62.

Sadka, E. 2006. "Public-Private Partnerships: A Public Economics Perspective." Working Paper Nr. 06/77. Washington, DC: IMF.

Saussier, S., C. Staropoli, and A. Yvrande-Billon, 2009. "Public-Private Agreements, Institutions, and Competition: When Economic Theory Meets Facts." *Review of Industrial Organization* 35, 1–18.

Savas, E., 2000. *Privatization and Public-Private Partnerships.* New York: Chatham House Publishers.

Schleifer, A., 1998. "State versus Private Ownership." *Journal of Economic Perspectives* 12, 133–150.

Schmidt, K., 1996a. "Incomplete Contracts and Privatization." *European Economic Review* 40, 569–580.

1996b. "The Costs and Benefits of Privatization: An Incomplete Contracts Approach." *Journal of Law, Economics and Organization* 12, 1–24.

Schwartz, G., A. Carbacho, and K. Funke, 2008. *Public Investment and Public-Private Partnerships*. Houndmills: Palgrave Macmillan.

Shugart, C., 2010. "PPPs, the Public Sector Comparator, and Discount Rates: Key Issues for Developing Countries," in D. F. Burgess and G. Jenkins (eds.), *Discount Rates for the Evaluation of Public Private Partnerships*. Kingston: John Deutsch Institute.

Small, K., 2010. "Private Provision of Highways: Economic Issues." *Transport Reviews* 30, 11–31.

Small, K., C. Winston, and C. Evans, 1989. *Road Work: A New Highway Pricing and Investment Policy*. Washington, DC: Brookings Institution.

Small, K. and E. Verhoef, 2007. *The Economics of Urban Transportation*. London: Routledge.

Spulber, D., 1989. *Regulation and Markets*. Cambridge, MA: MIT Press.

Starr, P. 1988. "The Meaning of Privatization." *Yale Law and Policy Review* 6, 6–41.

Stewart-Smith, M. 1995. "Private Financing and Infrastructure Provision in Emerging Markets." *Law and Policy in International Business* 26, 987–1011.

Stigler, George . 1968. *The Organization of Industry*. Homewood: Richard D. Irwin.

Tirole, J., 1997. "Comentarios a la propuesta de Engel, Fischer y Galetovic sobre licitación de carreteras." *Estudios Públicos* 65, 201–214.

2006. *The Theory of Corporate Finance*. Princeton, NJ: Princeton University Press.

Trujillo, J., R. Cohen, X. Freixas, and R. Sheehy, 1998. "Infrastructure Financing with Unbundled Mechanisms." *The Financier* 5, 10–27.

Tsekeris, T. and S. Voss, 2009. "Design and Evaluation of Road Pricing: State-of-the-Art and Methodological Advances." *Netnomics* 10, 5–52.

Ubbels, B. and E. Verhoef, 2008. "Auctioning Concessions for Private Roads." *Transportation Research Part A* 42, 5–72.

Vaillancourt-Roseneau, P. 2000. *Public-Private Policy Partnerships*. Cambridge, MA: MIT Press.

Välilä, T., 2005. "How Expensive Are Cost Savings? On the Economics of Public-Private Partnerships." *EIB Economic Studies* 10, 10–30.

Verhoef, E., 2007. "Second-Best Road Pricing through Highway Franchising." *Journal of Urban Economics* 62, 337–361.

2008. "Private Roads: Auctions and Competition in Networks." *Journal of Transport Economics and Policy* 42, 463–493.

Weber, B. and H. Alfen, 2010. *Infrastructure as an Asset Class: Investment Strategies, Project Finance and PPPs*. New York: John Wiley & Sons.

Williamson, O., 1976. "Franchise Bidding for Natural Monopoly: In General and with Respect to CATV." *Bell Journal of Economics* 7, 73–104.

1985. *The Economic Institutions of Capitalism*. New York: Free Press.

Wu, W., 2010. "Urban Infrastructure Financing and Economic Performance in China." *Urban Geography* 31, 648–667.

Yescombe, E. R., 2002. *Principles of Project Finance*. Burlington, VT: Academic Press.

2007. *Public-Private Partnerships: Principles of Policy and Finance*. Oxford: Butterworth-Heinemann.

Index

Printed in the United States
By Bookmasters